It's nearly impossible to define an 'Indian Indie', given how many diverse regional cultures India consists of, and how many distinct languages and paradigms Indie filmmakers create in. There is arguably no other country in the world whose independent cinema is as varied in textures and fabrics and socio-cultural nuances as India's is. It takes an unparalleled depth of insight and a tenacious spirit to attempt to bring all of these together into the pages of a single book, where one can begin to understand what makes the New Independent Indian Cinema so unique.

Devashish Makhija, Director, *Ajji*, *Bhonsle*

A pioneering work on a neglected area of India's vibrant cinema. Ashvin Devasundaram's timely new book is a much-needed addition to the academic studies of the world's largest film factory. With its lively case studies and accessible writing style, the book will be a valuable resource for researchers and students interested in world cinema.

Daya Thussu, Professor of International Communication,
Hong Kong Baptist University

Indian Indies

This book offers a concise and cutting-edge repository of essential information on new independent Indian films, which have orchestrated a recent renaissance in the Bollywood-dominated Indian cinema sphere.

Spotlighting a specific timeline, from the Indies' consolidated emergence in 2010 across a decade of their development, the book takes note of recent transformations in the Indian political, economic, cultural and social matrix and the concurrent release of unflinchingly interrogative and radically evocative films that traverse LGBTQ+ issues, female empowerment, caste discrimination, populist politics and religious violence.

A combination of essential Indie-specific information and concise case studies makes this a must-have quick guide to the future torchbearers of Indian cinema for scholars, students, early career researchers and a global audience interested in intersecting aspects of cinema, culture, politics and society in contemporary India.

Ashvin Immanuel Devasundaram is Senior Lecturer in World Cinema at Queen Mary University of London. He is author of *India's New Independent Cinema: Rise of the Hybrid* (2016) and editor of *Indian Cinema Beyond Bollywood: The New Independent Cinema Revolution* (2018). Ashvin is Associate Director of the UK Asian Film Festival – London and has directed the UK Heritage Lottery-funded documentary *Movies, Memories, Magic* (2018).

Routledge Focus on Film Studies

Figure 0.1 Sushama Deshpande in *Ajji*, directed by Devashish Makhija (2017)
Source: Film still reproduced with the director's permission

Indian Indies

A Guide to New Independent
Indian Cinema

Ashvin Immanuel Devasundaram

with a foreword by Shabana Azmi

LONDON AND NEW YORK

First published 2022
by Routledge
4 Park Square, Milton Park, Abingdon, Oxon OX14 4RN

and by Routledge
605 Third Avenue, New York, NY 10158

Routledge is an imprint of the Taylor & Francis Group, an informa business

© 2022 Ashvin Immanuel Devasundaram

British Library Cataloguing-in-Publication Data
A catalogue record for this book is available from the British Library

Library of Congress Cataloging-in-Publication Data
A catalog record for this book has been requested

ISBN: 978-0-367-54374-7 (hbk)
ISBN: 978-0-367-54375-4 (pbk)
ISBN: 978-1-003-08900-1 (ebk)

DOI: 10.4324/9781003089001

Typeset in Times New Roman
by Apex CoVantage, LLC

This book is dedicated to John Field, who makes my world go around.

Contents

Foreword

This book comes at a crucial point in the timeline of Indian cinema when bold, dynamic and exciting changes are being galvanised by a new breed of independent films. Acknowledging the radical changes sparked by new independent Indian cinema over 2010–21, this book provides an essential and meticulous overview of the new Indian Indies. Devasundaram's book presents a probing and kaleidoscopic insight into current affairs and pertinent issues ranging from feminist and LGBTQ+ themes, caste-discrimination and religion-based politics to the practical side of exhibition and distribution. This book will serve as an enriching and enlightening guide for all readers interested in the new face of Indian cinema.

Shabana Azmi

Acknowledgements

This title was conceived during the course of a difficult Covid-19 pandemic year, when devastation and loss became the universal norm. This book is a small tribute to my mother Hilda Devasundaram – my foremost inspiration and leading light. I am deeply indebted to Shabana Azmi – a veritable icon of Indian cinema, for her gracious contribution of the foreword. I would like to thank Deepshi Singh for her enthusiastic and assiduous assistance towards compiling the appendix list of independent Indian films. I am also grateful to Dr Pushpinder Chowdhry and Amandeep Dhillon for all their support. Thanks to my siblings and their families – Bina, Avinash, Renji, Nithya, Ria, Shreya, Leah and Yohan for all the love and solidarity during a most difficult year. Thanks to Mohan Uncle for sending interesting and useful archive and news articles my way. I am grateful to Suzanne Richardson and Tanushree Baijal at Routledge for all their help. Most of all, to my imperturbable husband, John, whose love, wisdom, support and intellectual sparring ensure my scholarly and philosophical forays remain lively, vibrant, fulfilling and passionate. This book is inspired by and therefore owes a debt of gratitude to intrepid independent filmmakers, artists, musicians, writers, journalists, scholars, students, teachers, activists, rationalists and all other individuals who in their own little ways challenge authoritarian systems, discriminatory practices, religious fundamentalism and sociopolitical injustice in the hope of orchestrating change and fostering freedom for all.

Introduction

The new wave of independent Indian cinema has traversed a decade since its rise to prominence around 2010, as a distinctly different cohort of Indian films. Following in the footsteps of my monograph *India's New Independent Cinema: Rise of the Hybrid* in 2016 and edited anthology *Indian Cinema Beyond Bollywood: The New Independent Cinema Revolution* in 2018, this book affords the opportunity to cast a contemporary eye over the state of the Indian Indies in 2021. Monumental global events such as the Covid-19 pandemic in 2020–21 and tumultuous upheavals in the Indian political landscape render this a timely moment to reassess the role of alternative independent Indian films in breaking the dominant Bollywood mould through innovation in film form, style and espousal of unconventional content.

This title aims to recontextualise and render to a broader readership foundational facets of my previous scholarly work on new independent Indian cinema. Significantly, the book will present fresh perspectives, facts and details, taking into account new and ongoing developments, films, filmmakers, the digital turn and vicissitudes in current affairs. This book therefore endeavours to serve as a bespoke contemporary, concise and accessible resource, fully-focused on new independent Indian cinema (2010–21).

In my research and literature on new independent Indian cinema, I have deployed deliberately the capitalised form – 'Indies' – to delineate these films from the globally generic term 'indies' and also to acknowledge the unique role of contemporary alternative new wave films in transforming the topography of Indian cinema spanning 2010–21. Similarly, in this book, I use quotation marks to challenge the basis, validity and justifiability of caste differentiation and its subordinating terminology – so-called 'upper-caste' and 'lower-caste' in contemporary India. This is a small gesture to demonstrate that discrimination on the basis of race, gender, religion, ethnicity, sexual orientation and caste inter alia are unacceptable on semiotic and linguistic as well as conceptual, socio-political and performative levels – especially pertinent to the ongoing socio-political climate in India.

DOI: 10.4324/9781003089001-1

A plethora of influential and high-profile Indies have been released in recent years that are entangled in shapeshifting social, economic, cultural and political events in the Indian landscape. A number of emerging and established Indian and global scholars are engaging with the new paradigm shift in Indian cinema, and through their research, assisting the development of an independent sub-area of Indian cinema studies beyond the restrictive confines of Bollywood. Dynamic new research by Jayjit Sarkar and Anik Sarkar (2023), Harmanpreet Kaur (2021), Smith Mehta (2019) and Priyanka Verma (2020) attests to an emerging generation of scholars engaging with ongoing, unfolding and understudied aspects of the new Indian cinema terrain. The intensifying output of scholarly literature, specifically on Indie films and discourses interpreted by these films in tandem with the evolution and development of the new independent Indian film sector, indicates the future direction of travel of Indian film studies and Indian cinema.

It is precisely the discursive and interrogative nature of new wave independent Indian cinema that necessitates a holistic approach, accounting for the intersectional and interdisciplinary local, national and global grid in which the new Indies are enmeshed. India's democratic credentials are facing an existential crisis with the seemingly ineluctable rise of a neofascist majoritarian governmental model committed to dismantling the nation's secular socio-political fabric and establishing a theocratic Hindu *rashtra* (nation). The latter half of the recent decade has witnessed intensifying levels of intolerance, mob vigilantism, attacks on religious minorities, women, journalists, activists, rationalists, academics, farmers, Dalits, Adivasis, and most conspicuously, the normalisation of Hindu supremacist ideology amongst significant swathes of the Indian demographic, particularly in BJP-governed states. Dissenting and critical voices in the academic sphere have also fallen under an authoritarian censuring gaze. In this environment of endangerment, not only of free speech and expression, but also of India's democratic and constitutional credentials, new independent films have grappled consistently with turbulent and transformative events in the nation's zeitgeist. New state censorship regulations introduced in 2020–21 pose a discernible future threat to culturally and politically outspoken Indie films. Their hitherto creative freedom to disseminate in uncensored form in the digital domain now faces surveillance, control and proscription by the ruling state apparatus.

For the moment, the Indies continue to gain visibility on national and global levels through the international film festival circuit and the potent proliferative digital streaming platforms of Netflix and Amazon Prime Video amongst others. This digital turn is a pivotal milestone in the Indies' journey across a decade as technological conduits of production, distribution and widening access have stimulated an expansive range of independent films that challenge the stereotypical and formulaic blueprint of mainstream Bollywood.

From the temporal vantage point of 2021, it is therefore the endeavour of this book to present a condensed and cutting-edge snapshot of the new Indies. It is hoped that this foundational, conceptual and practical guide to new independent Indian films will serve as a catalyst for scholars, practitioners, cultural curators and non-specialist aficionados of new Indian Indie cinema to shape and contribute to the rich and exciting discourse of contemporary Indie films as a distinctive dimension of Indian cinema.

References

Devasundaram, A. (2016). *India's new independent cinema: Rise of the hybrid.* New York: Routledge.

Devasundaram, A. (2018). *Indian cinema beyond Bollywood: The new independent cinema revolution.* New York: Routledge.

Kaur, H. (2021). At home in the world: Co-productions and Indian alternative cinema. *BioScope*, 11(2), SAGE, pp. 123–145.

Mehta, S. (2019). Precarity and new media: Through the lens of Indian creators. *International Journal of Communication*, 13, pp. 5548–5567.

Sarkar, J. and Sarkar, A., eds. (2023). *A handbook of Indian indie cinema.* London: Routledge.

Verma, P. (2020). Parched (sex and the village: An Indian version). *Free Associations: Psychoanalysis and Culture*, 79, pp. 112–120.

1 In the beginning
The birth of the new Indies

Overview

Filmmaker Dibakar Banerjee states: 'We need cinema that takes on, head on, the issues of, according to me, racism in India, independence from objectification of women, independence from jingoism, national jingoism, jingoism of the *Bharatiyata*, independence from organised religion' (Film Companion, 2021).

The emergence of a new wave of independent films constitutes a radical renaissance in contemporary Indian cinema. India's new 'Indies' began to gain prominence and visibility around 2010 – a watershed year in their evolutionary trajectory. In the millennial decade prior to 2010, the notion of independent films created outside or in opposition to Mumbai-based mainstream commercial Hindi cinema – Bollywood – was certainly not inconceivable or unprecedented. However, the alternative films released between 2000 and 2009 were relatively few and far between – disaggregated, impeded by inadequate funding, intermittent exhibition, limited distribution and niche audiences. At the time, the prospect of positioning these independent films as potential contenders to Bollywood's undisputed cinematic dominance was not given serious consideration. The release of several seminal Indie films in 2010, including *Peepli Live*, *Udaan*, *LSD: Love, Sex Aur Dhoka*, *Dhobi Ghat*, *I Am* and *Gandu*, gave credence to the conception of a bona fide alternative genre of independent films. Converging from the shards and sparks of sporadic film releases in the early stages of the millennium into a cohesive, consistent, cross-regional, multilingual, impactful and increasingly prolific film form, the idea of a *new wave* of Indian 'Indies' took root.

These Indie films were distinctly different from standard Bollywood blockbusters, displaying diversity of form, style and, most conspicuously, unconventional and eclectic content. An ever-increasing number of these films started emerging from across multiple Indian urban centres, revealing

DOI: 10.4324/9781003089001-2

multi-dimensional sides of India seldom represented in Bollywood. Topical Indie film themes span gender-based violence, female-centric perspectives, LGBTQ+ rights, unregulated neoliberalism, predatory capitalism, caste-discrimination, child labour, human trafficking, religious fundamentalism, social and political repression of ethnic and religious minorities, economic inequality, state corruption, authoritarian law enforcement practices, and malfunctioning legal and judicial systems. In hindsight of a decade since their largely unobtrusive but silently revolutionary rise to prominence in 2010, the Indies are now a mainstay in the Indian filmmaking firmament. It would therefore be a cardinal error to continue the entrenched tendency, especially prevalent in western cultural perspectives, of collapsing all forms of Indian cinema and culture into Bollywood. To persist with this undifferentiating approach entails failure to take heed of the monumental transformations and paradigm shifts galvanised by Indian Indie cinema not to mention the decolonising currents in the global academy. Since their emergence as a new wave and increasing affiliation with the international web streaming distributive infrastructure of Netflix and Amazon Prime Video, the Indies continue to reconceptualise and reimagine Indian cinema. Indeed, the Indies have instigated Bollywood itself to refurbish, reorient and reassess its own conventional strategies and formulaic idioms of film form, style and content.

Spanning over a decade of the Indies' emergence (2010–21), this chapter extends a condensed, contextual insight into the provenance and evolution of the Indies. It will appraise the multiple meanings of the term 'Indian Indie' to reveal some of the idiosyncratic and paradoxical characteristics of these new independent films. This chapter will identify the Indies' links to other previous forms of Indian cinema, particularly the influential but short-lived Parallel cinema movement of the 1970s–'80s, itself heralded as 'new wave' Indian cinema at the time. Ultimately, the new Indies which are the focus of this book will be framed as a postmodern, pan-Indian and polylingual phenomenon, thereby highlighting the intrinsic diversity of this contemporary new wave of independent films.

Multiple meanings of indie: What are the new Indian Indies?

Films with alternative content and storylines that stand apart from conventional, predictable and melodramatic Bollywood song and dance romance and action extravaganzas are regarded broadly as 'independent' in the Indian context. Director of the independent film *B.A. Pass* (2012), Ajay Bahl defines the Indian Indie as a 'reaction to Bollywood' that 'thrives on its non-confirmation of that style', and therefore reflects the binary template

'Bollywood versus Independent Indian Cinema' (Bhambra, 2017). Indeed, Indian Indie films are often positioned on the opposite pole to Bollywood. Whilst this may be valid on ideological, conceptual, perceptive and thematic levels, the colossal expansiveness, innate diversity and interconnectedness of the multifarious *cinemas* of India call for a more critical, nuanced and less binary understanding of the Indie new wave.

One of the crucial considerations in any in-depth investigation of the independent new wave relates to the challenging task of defining the new Indian Indies. As shapeshifting, multifaceted, hybrid, fluid, flexible and adaptable films, the new Indies defy and destabilise attempts to compartmentalise them into easily predictable categories. The independent filmmaking sector in India lacks a dedicated funding, exhibition and distribution infrastructure. Filmmakers therefore are assiduous in seeking wider audiences and box-office success which determines their ability to create a subsequent film. In this sense, as will be observed later in this chapter, the new wave of Indian Indies is distinctly different from the previous 'new wave' of arthouse cinema called the Parallel cinema movement of the 1970s and '80s. As children of the digital age cutting their filmmaking teeth in the crucible of globalisation, for the most part, contemporary Indian Indie filmmakers are keenly invested in the commercial viability, magnified visibility and marketability of their films. It is not uncommon for Indie filmmakers to seek the participation of a high-profile mainstream Bollywood star actor, gain the patronage of a Bollywood film producer or celebrity, or align with a mainstream commercial production house. On a conceptual level, semiotic use of the term 'Indie' in the Indian cinema matrix is therefore stylised, culturally specific, circumstantial and expedient. In the Indian context, the term 'Indie' does not automatically refer to films made outside the mainstream studio system or with independent funding.

Whilst acknowledging its variable nature when transposed to an Indian cinema context, the malleable term 'Indie' is nonetheless a utilitarian, accommodating and adaptable reference point. The idiosyncratic Indian conception and usage of the appellation 'Indie' therefore comes with the concept-level caveat that the signifier – 'Indie' must always be multiple, contingent, context-dependent, versatile and pliable.

Renowned scholars and film critics have adduced multiple monikers to 21st century Indian films that are not archetypically Bollywood. These terms include '*hatke*/multiplex' (Dwyer, 2011), 'urban fringe' (Mazumdar, 2010) and 'Mindie' (Shedde). There have also been attempts to subsume the new Indies in appropriating and reductive nomenclature such as 'New Bollywood' (Gopal, 2011; Gehlawat, 2015), thereby denying the Indie new wave its own identity and agency. Following the radical turn effected by the cohesive and prolific emergence of independent Indian films since

2010, the term 'Indie' is now the commonly adopted generic signifier for the new wave of Indian independent films that have flowed with increasing abundance across a decade. Indeed, the accommodating and relatively unrestrictive term 'Indie' combines the specific Indian context of its usage with a vision of free-flowing, evolving alternative pathways towards expressing creative independence. This fusion of flexibility and specificity in the bespoke term Indian 'Indie' renders 'Indie' a suitable shorthand to refer to the new wave's heterogenous contemporary melting pot of film form, style and content. Indeed, deployment of the functional moniker 'Indian Indies' traverses the timeline of their evolution since 2010 and has been visible in news articles (Verma, 2011), academic scholarship (Devasundaram, 2016, 2018), bespoke websites such as India Independent Films.com (IIF) dedicated to charting and analysing the new wave (IIF, 2021) and the film festival circuit (Raindance.org, 2015).

In adopting the title 'Indian Indie', it is imperative to distinguish between the western and Indian conceptions of what 'Indie' entails. Independent cinema in the west refers largely to films funded, produced and distributed outside the mainstream studio system, although even this western paradigm has been destabilised in recent years. In the contemporary Indian cinema context, Indie films are not necessarily or always created and proliferated autonomously from mainstream commercial production companies, exhibitors and distributors. This is a singular feature of the Indian Indies. Due to the lack of a dedicated infrastructural system to support the independent filmmaking sector, several Indie directors often have no recourse but to align with conventional or mainstream sources of funding, marketing, exhibition and distribution in order to bring their film ideas to fruition. This 'privileged' class of Indies benefits from relatively bigger production budgets which facilitate more polished aesthetics, slick production values, amplified publicity and wider exhibition and dissemination opportunities. Good examples include two foundational Indies – *Peepli Live* and *Dhobi Ghat* from 2010, which were produced by Bollywood star Aamir Khan's eponymous production house AKP (Aamir Khan Productions) and the UTV Motion Pictures (now acquired by The Walt Disney Company India). This once again invokes the idea of the Indian Indies as spanning a spectrum – ranging from films that affiliate with mainstream production and distribution sources to films that are more 'genuinely' independent through autonomous and alternative modes of finance, creation and dissemination.

This stratified system is therefore punctuated by several Indian Indies that reject, circumvent or are unable to forge strategic alliances with dominant commercial conduits of film finance, exhibition, distribution and promotion. A range of Indies such as *Harud*, *Gandu*, *I Am* (all from 2010), *Miss Lovely* (2012), *Kothanodi/The River of Fables* (2015), *Haanduk/*

The Hidden Corner (2016), *Lucia* (2013), *Shreelancer* (2017) and *Village Rockstars* (2018) are often self-funded, crowdfunded or brought into being via other alternative local, national and international sponsorship and co-production strategies outside the mainstream studio ecosystem.

Once again, this attests to the diverse types – a broad spectrum or even a tier-system of Indie films, under the overarching classification new 'Indian Indies'. Essentially, 'Indie' in the Indian context is not always positioned automatically outside the orbit and influence of the dominant Bollywood industry. The foundational or determining criterion that distinguishes an Indian Indie from a Bollywood film is alternative, unorthodox, realist, radical or controversial thematic *content*. Film critic Anupama Chopra emphasises this dimension of the Indian Indies: 'we're not talking about finance or distribution, but content and storytelling. These films don't adhere to the song-and-dance formula we've had for many years' (Sakula, 2015).

Unlike Bollywood's formulaic approach that invariably privileges escapist entertainment and economic profit, Indian Indie films can afford filmmakers a more autonomous personal vision and relatively uncompromising voice in relation to espousing both experimental and entertaining formal and stylistic approaches whilst representing unusual topical content. As the iconoclast of the Indian Indie filmmaking domain – controversial director Q (Qaushik Mukherjee) – asserts, 'an indie is always an exercise to be free of any hostile or disruptive forces during the film's creation' (Dasgupta, 2012).

In a candid talking-heads documentary, *The Other Way* (Dasgupta and Sethumadhavan, 2014) shared on YouTube, an ensemble of new wave Indie directors including Q, Onir, Vasan Bala, Kenny Basumatary, Gitanjali Rao and Pawan Kumar demonstrate that the diverse definitions of Indie correspond to the intrinsically broad bandwidth of Indie films that range and vary in form, style, cross-regional provenance, budgetary, logistical and distributive resources. The commentators reveal the trials, tribulations and travails faced by aspiring and upcoming filmmakers. In India's Bollywood-dominated landscape, alternative film creators often have to resort to DIY and improvisational filmmaking approaches, deploying outside of the box and off-the-cuff mechanisms and strategies to work around financial and logistical deficits. This invokes comparisons with the uniquely Indian phenomenon of *jugaad* – an everyday lived practice especially amongst underprivileged subaltern classes. As Amit Rai (2019) notes, *jugaad* involves the intuitive adoption of 'workarounds and hacks to solve problems', making the best of meagre immediately available resources and strategies to transform ostensibly useless objects into something workable and functional. The aforementioned independent filmmakers harness *The Other Way* as a self-reflexive documentary platform to reveal important information about the formative state of the Indian independent film sector in 2012, highlighting the need to experiment, improvise and innovate within mitigating circumstances and operate with a restricted toolkit to create 'beauty out of chaos'.

There has been a radical rupture since the aforementioned filmmakers shared their insights into the often beleaguered infrastructural state of play in Indian Indie filmmaking, which had been hampered by elusive funding and dissemination avenues. This metamorphosis has emerged significantly through the entry in 2016 of Netflix and Amazon Prime Video into the Indian market, marking the general rise of more than 40 'OTT' (over-the-top) streaming platforms in India by 2020. The two global web streaming leviathans have played a particularly pivotal role in filling the funding, exhibition and distribution vacuum for non-Bollywood independent films, and have largely adopted the mantle of de facto Indie infrastructure via the digital domain. This is ironic, considering the global corporate ethos of both Netflix and Amazon Prime Video. In this context, Aparna Acharekar, programming head of Zee5 India, explains the shifting pattern of independent film proliferation:

> Cinema theatres are a medium for mass entertainment and big-budget films. On the other hand, OTT is the perfect medium for small, independent cinema. Every kind of film is empowered and celebrated here with no scope for monopolies.
>
> (Kavitha, 2020)

The lockdown scenario arising from the global Covid-19 pandemic in 2020 has consolidated the amplifying influence of video-on-demand digital platforms, devolving further the Indian Indies' former reliance on exhibition in cinema multiplexes and film festivals. According to a Broadcast Audience Research Council India and Nielsen report, OTT web streaming portals witnessed 'more than a 50 per cent rise in time spent watching movies on their platforms in April as compared with pre-Covid times' (Kavitha, 2020). The diverse mechanisms of Indie funding, distribution and exhibition will be discussed in more depth in Chapter 5.

Encapsulating the points raised so far, the rule of thumb is to acknowledge and affirm the innate heterogeneity of the Indian Indie new wave whilst applying the fluid and functional term 'Indie' as a signifier that rebels against any totalising signified meaning. The answer to the vexed question of Indian Indie classification lies in the diffuse varieties of Indie films that share a commonality of thematic content that is radically divergent from Mumbai-centric Bollywood. In essence, there are multiple modes of being 'Indie' in the contemporary Indian cinema terrain. We will now consider some of the other distinctive characteristics of the new wave Indies that differentiate them from Bollywood but also demonstrate their dialogic relationship with the dominant commercial cinema form. These Indie traits include unconventional content, hybridity, *glocality* and linguistic diversity.

Unconventional content: topical themes and issues

The Indies' intrinsic hybridity of form, style and content is shaped by their status as self-critical film interpreters of a polarised postmodern Indian era of globalisation and religion-based majoritarian politics. India's contemporary template of conjoined neoliberalism and divisive Hindu nationalism has been the priority of Narendra Modi's BJP regime since its landslide election victory in 2014 and re-election in 2019. Against the backdrop of this plunge into Hindutva-based populism, the independent film sector in India is enmeshed in a discursive network of digital hyperreality, consumer culture and India's aspiration to achieve global economic superpower status in the 21st century. Whilst Bollywood narratives tend to validate this majoritarian nationalist and neoliberal status quo, the Indies largely seek to interrogate the conflicting, contradictory, unpredictable and splintering aspects of India's immersion into the postmodern digital age.

The Indies engage with diverse socio-political thematic content, often from intersectional perspectives spanning gender, sexuality, caste, religion, politics, urban and rural divisions, socio-economic inequalities and other polemical issues. Importantly, Indie stories are mostly told from the point of view of ordinary, marginalised or oppressed individuals and social groups including women, religious minorities, Dalits, Adivasis (tribals), LGBTQ+ and differently-abled people. Unlike Bollywood's privileging of affluent and aspirational upper-class and middle-class lifestyles, Indies are more invested in subaltern perspectives of the powerless and peripheralized who reside in the shadowlands of contemporary Indian society. In summary, the fundamental point of distinction between the Indies and Bollywood is divergent content underpinned by multidimensional formal and stylistic approaches. The next chapter provides a detailed exploration of the Indies' engagement with specific themes and issues that constitute a distinct departure from mainstream commercial cinema content.

Hybridity

Products of India's postmodern condition

Postmodern elements of pastiche and bricolage – pasting together disparate elements of form, style and narrative themes into experimental collages of free play with non-linear time and space – have been evident in the Indies across the decade since their rise to prominence. Postmodern hybridity is a hallmark of several new wave Indies from *Gandu* (2010) and *Island City* (2015) to *Toofan Mail* (2021). The oneiric aesthetic of Akriti Singh's *Toofan Mail* is a whimsical yet critical evocation of several political timelines in Indian history. Aditya Vikram Sengupta's Bengali film *Jonaki* (2018) adopts meticulous formalism alongside surreal and immersive visual images that coalesce in a painterly canvas of memory, time and space – a strategy mirrored in Akshay Indikar's Marathi film *Sthalpuran/Chronicle of Space* (2020).

Several Indies tap directly into India's immersion into the postmodern condition in terms of the country's hypernormalisation of consumerism, commodification, technologisation and urbanisation coterminous with alienating consequences and widening of socio-economic disparities. India's turbulent tug-of-war between spiritualism and modernity, tradition and neoliberalism informs the Indies' approach to capturing the mood of the nation's many social, cultural, political and religious traumas, tensions and anxieties. Invoking the postmodern era's hypervisuality and omnipresence of media in all its conventional and digital avatars, several Indies deploy the aesthetics of gaming, webcams, surveillance cameras, social media, music videos and smartphones, to embellish narratives in films such as *LSD: Love, Sex aur Dhoka*, (Dibakar Banerjee, 2010), *Ship of Theseus* (Anand Gandhi, 2012), *Aligarh* (Hansal Mehta, 2016), *Masaan/Crematorium* (Neeraj Ghaywan, 2015) and *Kalla Notam/The False Eye* (Rahul Riji Nair, 2020). Blending and subverting genre conventions, meta-referential films such as Kabir Mehta's *Buddha.mov* (2017) and Kabir Chowdhry's *Mehsampur* (2018) blur boundaries of the biopic, documentary and docufiction formats.

Indies harness consistently the often interchangeable mosaic, portmanteau, anthology and hyperlink film formats featuring either a compendium of short story segments (anthology) or multiple intersecting storylines (hyperlink) set in cosmopolitan cities and smaller towns. Examples include early Indie films such as *I Am* and *Dhobi Ghat* in 2010 to later films such as *Masaan* (2015), *X: Past is Present* (2015), *Ship of Theseus* (2012), *Teenkahon/Three Obsessions* (2014), *Lipstick Under My Burkha* (2016), *Super Deluxe* (2019), *Kathaah@8* (2019) and the Netflix anthology *Ajeeb Daastaans* (2021). Neeraj Ghaywan, director of *Geeli Pucchi/Sloppy Kisses* one of four story instalments in *Ajeeb Daastaans*, emphasises the importance of engaging with narratives that reveal the 'intersection of identities' asserting how 'it is essential for us to see people with fused identities and not see their subaltern selves in silos' (Singh, 2021).

The idea of the postmodern city in film has largely been dominated by Eurocentric perspectives in popular culture and in scholarly literature such as *From Moscow to Madrid: Postmodern Cities, European Cinema* (Mazierska and Rascaroli, 2003). In this context, the new Indies present a Global South interpretation of an urban India in motion, redolent with technological interfaces, rampant consumerism and a chaotic network society (Castells, 1996) enmeshed in global cultural flows (Appadurai, 1990). This leitmotif of the postmodern city is invoked in a gamut of Indies spanning *I Am*, *Dhobi Ghat*, *B.A. Pass* and *Photograph* that deal with ruptures, subversion, human encounters, coincidence and shared trauma in the cityscape (Narine, 2010, p. 216).

Unlike their non-commercial Parallel cinema predecessors in India's socialist era of the 1970s–'80s, contemporary new Indie filmmakers are impelled significantly to enhance the regional, national and global visibility of their films through assiduous promotion and marketing. Targeting a modicum of box-office success or gaining some financial recompense is a survival strategy for the Indies in an arena monopolised by Bollywood. Since 2010, the prevailing Indian zeitgeist of market-driven economic imperatives and dearth of funding for films with alternative content has spurred several independent directors to align with mainstream Bollywood-oriented production and distribution houses such as Eros International (*Aligarh*), Yash Raj Films (*Titli*) and Ajay Devgn FFilms (*Parched*) for funding and distribution.

Bollywood personalities and celebrities are also enlisted to 'present' or promote Indie films in a phenomenon that resembles a 'godparent' syndrome (Devasundaram, 2016, p. 84). In this sense, Kiran Rao, wife (at the time) of Bollywood star Aamir Khan, presented *Ship of Theseus*; Ajay Devgn was the patron for *Parched*; Karan Johar promoted *The Lunchbox* and co-produced *Ajeeb Daastaans*; and Vivek Oberoi was one of the producers of *Dekh Indian Circus* (2011). These expedient alliances with Bollywood may seem antithetical to the essence of the term 'Indie'. Importantly, not all Indian Indie new wave productions align strategically with Bollywood structures – several nationally and globally recognised regional language independent films from outside the Mumbai space, particularly Marathi, Tamil, Bengali, Malayalam, Assamese and Manipuri, are seldom linked to the Bollywood industry.

In a further demonstration of hybridity in the Indie sector, it is not uncommon for alternative films, for example *Peepli Live*, *Masaan*, *Sairat* and *Haider*, to incept strategically in their narratives selected Bollywood tropes, such as song sequences and extra-diegetic musical overlays although the use of songs is more context-driven, parodic or transgressive in Indie narratives. Some Indie films insert intertextual references to Bollywood and its megastars (mention of Shah Rukh Khan in the independent film *Parched*,

Salman Khan in *Haider* and Amitabh Bachchan in *Tikli and Laxmi Bomb*), calling attention to the films' positioning outside Bollywood-dominated Indian popular culture.

The shapeshifting and strategic versatility of the Indies – their postmodern ability to morph, blend and adopt different styles and sensibilities to critique national grand narratives of 'traditional' Indian morals and values, socio-religious practices and political power – has also contributed to their transmutation into highly successful web series on Netflix and Amazon Prime Video. Prominent examples include *Sacred Games* (2018), *The Family Man* (2019), *Paatal Lok* (2020), *Tandav* (2021) *and Bombay Begums* (2021), all delving thematically into the taboo and topical netherworld of class, caste, religion, politics, systemic corruption and gender-based violence. These examples demonstrate how the new wave Indies with their left-of-field content have been the breeding ground for the expanded format of Indian web series on global streaming platforms. At the vanguard of these successful online series are actors, producers, directors and other creative personnel synonymous with the new wave of Indies since 2010. Notable figures include Anurag Kashyap, Avinash Arun, Vikramaditya Motwane, Alankrita Shrivastava, Guneet Monga, Radhika Apte, Tannishtha Chatterjee, Richa Chadda, Sanjay Mishra, Tillotama Shome, Nawazuddin Siddiqui, Neeraj Kabi, Geetanjali Kulkarni, Rajkummar Rao, Manoj Bajpayee, Adil Hussain, Plabita Borthakur, Shalini Vats and Rathna Shah Pathak.

Hybrid casting: non-professional actors and mainstream stars

Hybridity is also coded into Indie strategies of casting actors, which akin to the multidimensional nature of the Indie new wave, can amalgamate diverse approaches. Notably, several alternative filmmakers endeavour to enlist the support of Bollywood actors or producers to augment the visibility and public saleability of their films. This aspect of hybridity in the Indies in terms of occasionally forging strategic alliances with the powerful Bollywood industry is often a contingent necessity for Indies to gain wider audiences, optimise publicity and enhance exhibition opportunities. This once again invokes the idea of the new Indies as spanning a spectrum – from films that affiliate with mainstream production and distribution sources to films that are 'genuinely' independent through autonomous and alternative modes of creation and dissemination. Bollywood actors and producers often regard the Indie sector as 'worthy', cerebral and a conduit to gaining greater gravitas by associating with unconventional films that contain 'serious' and meaningful themes and issues.

For example, Bollywood star Shahid Kapoor was cast as the eponymous protagonist in *Haider* – Vishal Bharadwaj's visceral Kashmir-set adaptation of Shakespeare's *Hamlet*. Kapoor and Bollywood compatriot Alia Bhatt fronted *Udta Punjab* – a visceral and controversial film about a drug abuse crisis amongst young people in Punjab. Kunal Kapoor featured in *Noblemen* (2018) which dealt with the taboo topic of homosexuality and bullying in an elite boarding school. Other notable examples of Bollywood stars in hybrid Indie films include Aamir Khan in *Dhobi Ghat*, Vidya Balan in *Kahaani* (2012) *and Sherni* (2021), Amitabh Bachchan in *Pink* (2016) and Ayushmann Khurrana in *Article 15* (2019). This interpenetration between mainstream Bollywood and the independent space on the level of casting indicates not only hybridity but also situational expediency.

Several Indian Indies adhere to the conventional 'Indie' casting of non-professional, debutant or lesser-known local actors. For instance, *Harud* and *Side A and Side B* set in trouble-torn geopolitically-disputed Kashmir feature a cast of fledgling indigenous Kashmiri actors. The main protagonist of ground-breaking Indie *Peepli Live*, Omkar Das Manikpuri, has a background in local folk theatre and is the son of a daily wage labourer. Similarly, *Thithi*, a low-budget Kannada language film from the southern state of Karnataka, features an entire cast of local villagers. The film went on to win the Golden Leopard Award at the Locarno International Film Festival in 2015. Chaitanya Tamhane's *The Disciple* also features first-time actors Arun Modak and Arun Dravid.

The Indie space has been enriched by its own pantheon of dedicated Indie-focused stars who often specialise in Indie films sometimes making the odd foray into mainstream Bollywood. Rahul Bose is one of the pioneers of the independent sphere since his debut appearance in Dev Benegal's Hinglish low-budget film *English August* in 1994. Bose also starred alongside Konkona Sen Sharma – daughter of art cinema auteur Aparna Sen – in *Mr. and Mrs. Iyer* (2002). Sen Sharma is also synonymous with the new Indie space as an actor in films such as *Lipstick Under My Burkha* and *Dolly Kitty and the Twinkling Stars* (2020) and her directorial debut – *A Death in the Gunj* (2019). Rajkummar Rao is another widely recognised actor in several prominent Indies including *Gangs of Wasseypur* (2012), *Aligarh* (2015), *Trapped* (2016) and *Newton* (2017) whilst also foraying into Bollywood and Indie hybrid films such as *Ek Ladki Ko Dekha Toh Aisa Laga/How I Felt when I Saw that Girl* (2019) and *Stree* (2018).

Mirroring strong roles for women in the Indie sector, prolific and versatile female actors include Tannishtha Chatterjee in *Dekh Indian Circus*, *Angry Indian Goddesses*, *Jhalki* and *Chauranga*; Tillotama Shome whose notable work includes *Qissa*, *Sir* and *Raahgir/The Wayfarers*; and Kalki Koechlin in *That Girl in Yellow Boots*, *Margarita With a Straw* and *Waiting*.

Radhika Apte has also been a particularly productive contributor to several influential Indies including *I Am*, *Parched* and *Phobia* alongside a range of regional and mainstream Indian and international films and web series.

Glocality

During the inchoate stages, around 2010, of the new wave Indian Indies' development, several notable Indie film directors from Anand Gandhi to Kiran Rao affirmed the magnified exposure to global cinemas afforded Indian filmmakers and audiences through peer-to-peer filesharing torrent downloads, film festivals and satellite television channels (Devasundaram, 2014). This amplified awareness of global films alongside widening arenas of access to digital filmmaking and editing equipment contributed to a hybridised approach to cinema creation amongst young filmmakers in India.

Whilst Bollywood tends to have culturally specific grammar, codes, tropes and idioms, the new Indies could be perceived as *glocal* – melding a global 'world cinemas' aesthetic in terms of form and style with local thematic content rooted in Indian contexts. Local meets global on several levels in Indian Indie films. It is possible to identify in the Indies a pan-global assortment of styles and influences ranging from Akira Kurosawa, Jean-Luc Godard, Gaspar Noé, Ingmar Bergman, Stanley Kubrick, Majid Majidi, Mohsen Makhmalbaf, Takashi Miike to Kim Ki-duk. Coterminous with these international elements in the Indies' filmic physiology is the influence of previous Indian arthouse film movements and iconic Indian film directors.

For instance, the syncretic property of the Indies linking the local to the global invokes connections between India's preeminent postcolonial arthouse director Satyajit Ray and his Swedish auteur contemporary Ingmar Bergman. Intersections between the oeuvre, aesthetic strategies and film philosophies of these two filmmaking luminaries can be identified in contemporary Indian independent films such as *Ship of Theseus* (2012) and *Dear Molly* (2018) (Devasundaram, 2021). Indeed, the new Indian Indie sector paid homage to Satyajit Ray in his birth centenary year 2021 through the Netflix anthology film *Ray* based on the auteur's short stories.

The glocal facet of the Indies' hybridity is manifested in multiple Indie approaches to engaging with micro-level Indian themes and issues through a more universal cinematic grammar of form and style. This has augmented the Indies' transferability to online web streaming platforms such as Netflix and Amazon Prime Video. The global relatability of films with locally attuned Indian content such as *The Lunchbox* has precipitated recognition and financial success on an international stage. The global-meets-local aspect of new Indian Indie cinema is not restricted to formal and stylistic visual aesthetic strategies. It also pertains to transglobal creative and commercial collaborations. Glocality beyond onscreen representation and aesthetic form can be considered in the following modes:

Strategic

Financial co-productions that bring together Indian and international economic resources to enable film production, distribution and exhibition of Indian Indie films. For example, *The Lunchbox* was selected for the NFDC Film Bazaar Screenwriters' Lab in 2011, and went on to be part of the CineMART, co-production market of the International Film Festival Rotterdam. An India-France-Germany co-production, the film involved co-producers with global cinema credentials including Bosnian director Danis Tanovic (*No Man's Land*, 2001), Cedomir Kolar and Karsten Stoeter epitomising international infusions in an Indian story with crossover appeal.

Creative

This facet involves collaborations in the filmmaking process including editing, scriptwriting, music, sound design, cinematography and direction. For instance, music for *The Lunchbox* was scored by German composer Max Richter and edited by John F. Lyons with sound by Michael Kaczmarek. The ethereal soundscape for Anand Gandhi's *Ship of Theseus* was crafted by Gabor Erdelyi, sound designer for several films by renowned Hungarian auteur Bela Tarr. The film's dialogue is a polyglot local-global synthesis of Arabic, English, Hindi, Marathi, Kannada and Swedish. The film's final story segment segues from Mumbai to Sweden and features local actors, underpinning the theme of local-global connections.

Transnational music collaborations in Indie films are accompanied by a rising new cohort of young Indian original film score composers including Alokananda Dasgupta (*Trapped*), Karan Kulkarni (*Aligarh*) and Sagar Desh (*A Death in the Gunj*) who have emerged from the new Indian Indie film sector since 2010. Emphasising these composers' preference for more globally synthesised and experimental filmic soundscapes, Sankhayan Ghosh notes how 'much of their work is in small, independent films that can afford to jettison the traditional song-driven format of Indian film music and are understated enough to not underline every emotion with overbearing background music' (Ghosh, 2017).

A detailed insight into glocal facets of strategic and creative co-production can be accessed in Chapter 5.

Linguistic diversity

One of the notable features of the Indies is their emergence from across the geographical length and breadth of the nation. In this regard, there have been a plethora of politically and socio-culturally critical films in Marathi, Tamil, Bengali, Malayalam, Kannada, Assamese and other regional Indian languages which transcend their respective state borders and therefore fall under the broader banner of nationally and internationally visible new independent films (see next section on the difference between regional film industries and new Indies in regional languages).

Hindi – the dominant language of northern India – has been the long-standing language of choice in Bollywood films. Indeed, political attempts to position Hindi as the national language have been a bone of contention especially in southern Indian states, which have resisted what they perceive as the unsolicited imposition of an unfamiliar language on states that have their own rich indigenous linguistic heritage of Tamil, Telugu, Kannada and Malayalam. The languages specific to each state are reflected in significant regional commercial film industries often patronisingly reduced to ersatz facsimiles of the term Bollywood – Kollywood (Tamil/Tamil Nadu), Sandalwood (Kannada/Karnataka), Mollywood (Malayalam/Kerala) and Tollywood (Telugu/Andhra Pradesh and Telangana).

In contrast to Bollywood's Mumbai-centric focus and Hindi-dominated linguistic sameness, one of the elemental characteristics of the new Indies is their multilingualism. This polyglot diversity not only testifies to the Indies' emergence from across the length and breadth of India but also corresponds to their poly-dimensional political, cultural and social perspectives and combination of specific sensibilities and diverse mores of their regions and localities of origin.

Anusha Rizvi, director of *Peepli Live*, a film that built the foundation for the new wave to blossom, asserts that her aim was indeed to decentralise the influence of Mumbai and its tacit omnipresence in the diegetic world of Bollywood films. She accomplished this by setting the action of her film in the rural hinterlands of Peepli, an obscure village in the central Indian state of Madhya Pradesh (fictionalised as Mukhya Pradesh in the film). This rural locale is juxtaposed with New Delhi as a contrapuntal theatre of action. Similarly, Anurag Kashyap's visceral and violent two-part coal mafia feud saga *Gangs of Wasseypur* (2012) is rooted in the rural 'badlands' of Dhanbad in Jharkand state.

Indian independent cinema has devolved significantly over the decade of its evolution, with Indie films such Nicholas Kharkongor's *Axone* (2020) – a film about a group of young friends from the North Eastern state of Nagaland living as migrant workers in New Delhi – exemplifying the de-regionalisation of several vernacular state language Indie films through wider national and global networks and portals of exhibition. Distributed by Netflix, *Axone* deploys North Eastern local languages – Khasi, Naga, Manipuri and Arunachali alongside Hindi and English – to portray the racism and xenophobic violence routinely faced by North Eastern people in the rest of India. Kubrickian Grand Guignol horror film *Nirvana Inn* (2019) – an unconventional form in Indian cinema – is another example of polylingualism in the Indies with Hindi, English and Assamese blended together in the screenplay.

Tamil films such as *Kaaka Mutaai/The Crow's Egg, K.D.* and *Visaranai*, India's entry to the Foreign Language section of the Oscars in 2015, are a handful of examples of regional Indian films that have gained global visibility. Similarly, the low-budget Malayalam film *Sudani from Nigeria* (Zakariya Mohammed, 2018) is set in the southern state of Kerala and charts the story of a young Nigerian immigrant who develops a strong bond with a local Malayali Muslim man under the common canopy of their passion for football. An array of Malayalam Indie films such as *Papilio Buddha, Bangalore Days, Angamaly Diaries, Jallikatu, Kalla Nottam/The False Eye, Joji* and *The Great Indian Kitchen* have all gained national and international exposure and acclaim thereby earmarking them as part of the new independent Indian wave.

Bolstered by a revered, vibrant and longstanding folk theatre tradition, contemporary Marathi independent films continue to contribute seminal films to the new wave of Indian Indies. Notable examples include *Court, Ajji, Killa, Sexy Durga, Fandry* and *Sairat* whilst *Lucia* and *Thithi* are definitive examples of Indie films in Kannada – the state language of Karnataka. Similarly, *Harud, No Fathers in Kashmir, Side A & Side B* and *Hamid*, films set in the politically volatile Kashmir region, adopt the local Kashmiri language interspersed with English and Hindi as appropriate to the context. This is distinctly different from Bollywood films that deploy Hindi as the exclusive language irrespective of regional location or contextual specificity.

As will be explained further on, these cross-regional Indian films could be considered part of the new wave of Indies not only due to their innovative and topical themes but also the level of exposure, visibility and attention they have gained beyond their regional state boundaries.

Tracing the genealogical roots of new Indian Indies

To trace the evolutionary roots of the new Indian Indies, it is essential to return to postcolonial Indian arthouse cinema which followed India's independence in 1947. The objective of illustrious post-independence film directors such as Satyajit Ray, Mrinal Sen, Bimal Roy and Ritwik Ghatak was to harness cinematic representation to steer the nation-building exercise towards a new social consciousness. As the fledgling secular democratic republic under its first Prime Minister Jawaharlal Nehru adopted the socialist model and the vision of a welfare state, the arthouse filmmakers infused their narratives with socially exigent topical themes and issues. Film content grappled with untouchability, the urban-rural divide, wealth disparity, gender-based discrimination and systemic corruption. Bimal Roy's *Do Bigha Zamin* (1953) and Satyajit Ray's *Pather Panchali* (1955) provided evocative portrayals of rural poverty and widened the pathway to international exposure of social realist Indian films paved by Chetan Anand's Cannes Film Festival Palme d'Or-winning *Neecha Nagar/Lowly City* in 1946.

Shades of this social realist approach can be seen in new Indian Indies and their own aesthetics of 'local realism' (Devasundaram, forthcoming in 2022) adopted as a template to guide the Indies' glocal approach to interpreting contemporary India in the postmodern digital age. In effect, wielding film as an implement to cast a realist critical eye on prevailing social, cultural, economic and political systems is a feature of the early arthouse cinema that has been inherited by the Indian Indie new wave.

However, the Indies' most conspicuous connection within the family tree of Indian cinema (figure 1.1), is their kinship with films from the Parallel cinema movement which commenced in 1969 with Mrinal

Figure 1.1 The ship of Indian cinemas

Source: *India's New Independent Cinema* (Devasundaram, 2016)

Sen's seminal *Bhuvan Shome* and continued till the mid-1980s when the Parallel cinema movement was eclipsed by commercial Hindi cinema which in the early 1990s was given the totalising classificatory term 'Bollywood'.

The new Indies' predecessors – the Indian Parallel cinema movement of the late 1960s–'80s – could to a significant extent be posited as the non-commercial Indian cinema sector's affirmation and reflection of radical Latin American filmmakers Fernando Solanas' and Octavio Getino's revolutionary Third Cinema manifesto (Guneratne, 2003, p. 21). Absorbing the Third Cinema ethos of a revolutionary socio-political form of filmmaking that contested systemic inequalities and critiqued established regimes of power, filmmakers such as Saeed Akhtar Mirza, Shyam Benegal, Mani Kaul and Kumar Shahani punctuated the Parallel cinema sector with films such as *Uski Roti/Our Daily Bread* (Mani Kaul, 1969), *Maya Darpan/Mirror of Illusion* (Kumar Shahani, 1972), *Nishant/Night's End* (Shyam Bengal, 1975), *Albert Pinto Ko Gussa Kyoon Aata Hai/What Makes Albert Pinto Angry?* (Saeed Akhtar Mirza, 1980) and *Mohan Joshi Hazir Ho!/Summons for Mohan Joshi* (Saeed Akhtar Mirza, 1984).

The unifying feature between the new Indies and Parallel films is their espousal of alternative content – socially conscious and politically interrogative storylines that address topical and pertinent issues of the day. Experimentation with film form and style is also a distinctive feature shared by these old and new Indian cinematic waves. The influence of Parallel cinema auteurs such as Mani Kaul and Kumar Shahani are identifiable in the formal framework of contemporary Indie filmmakers including Amit Datta, Gurvinder Singh and Chaitanya Tamhane. Gurvinder Singh's *Anhe Ghore Da Daan/Alms for a Blind Horse* (2011) is a filmic tribute to his mentor Mani Kaul whilst aesthetic similarities are evident in Pawan K. Shrivastava's Indie *Life of an Outcast* (2018) which is available on Netflix. Chaitanya's Tamhane's *The Disciple* (also on Netflix) reincarnates Kaul's documentary odes to esoteric forms of Indian classical music in *Dhrupad* (1983) and *Siddheshwari* (1990) – Kaul's biographical paean to eminent Hindustani classical singer Siddheshwari Devi.

How are the new Indian Indies different from parallel cinema?

As mentioned earlier, the Indies could be considered the contemporary cinematic cousins and postmodern reincarnation of their forebears from the Parallel cinema movement. The new Indies are also distinctly different in several ways.

Crafted in the crucible of a globalising economy, the mechanics of Indie funding, production and distribution are often enmeshed in the capitalistic market logic milieu in which Bollywood thrives. Overweening corporate structures in contemporary India constitute a key departure from the erstwhile socialist Indian political system in the 1970s and '80s that supported and celebrated arthouse films of the Parallel cinema movement as the de facto 'national cinema of India' (Gopal, 2011, p. 8). In this regard, the portrayal of self-critical political and social themes in Parallel films were largely patronised by the state through funding and distribution assistance via the National Film Development Corporation (NFDC). In a contemporary Indian political milieu, the rise of *Hindutva* right-wing religious politics under the saffron banner of the BJP and Narendra Modi has entailed the empowerment of a repressive censorship regime that has imposed restrictive and punitive measures on liberal, progressive, alternative, dissenting or critical content in an array of Indie films. It is noteworthy that the role and power of the Indian Censor Board, which operates formally as the Central Board of Film Certification (CBFC) under the Ministry of Information and Broadcasting, has magnified exponentially under BJP rule since 2014, in comparison with film regulation structures during the heydays of Parallel films in the 1970s and '80s. As will be examined in Chapter 3, new Indies have had close and tempestuous encounters with proponents of political power and the Indian Censor Board.

It could also be argued that the new Indies adopt more panoptic political and cinematic perspectives than their Parallel cinema predecessors to represent the everyday lived experiences of Indian citizens. The Indies embrace a broader glocal approach through postmodern devices of fragmentation, pastiche, experimentation with film form, style and non-linearity. Overall, the Indies undertake a more transgressive and confrontational interrogation of reactionary metanarratives and dogmatic religious, cultural and political discourses. This is aptly demonstrated by Alankrita Shrivastava's controversial film *Lipstick Under My Burkha* (2016) which harnesses comedy as a thin veneer to explicitly imagine female emancipation and castigate retrenched forms of patriarchy in India.

Whilst scholars such as Steven Rawle (2018, p. 65) analogise the Parallel new wave Indian films of the 1970s and '80s to Chinese fifth and sixth generation films including *Red Sorghum* (Zhang Yimou, 1987), *Temptress Moon* (Chen Kaige, 1996) and *Beijing Bicycle* (Wang Xiaoshuai, 2001), the new Indies espouse state of the nation stories more reminiscent of the trenchant British film ripostes to the Thatcherite regime in the 1980s, including *The Ploughman's Lunch* (Richard Eyre, 1983), *Letter to Brezhnev* (Chris Bernard, 1985), *My Beautiful Laundrette* (Stephen Frears, 1985), *High Hopes*

(Mike Leigh, 1988) and *Defence of the Realm* (David Drury, 1986). The contemporary Indian Indies are also reminiscent of a cohort of contemporary American independent films that unveil the fracturing reverberations of Reaganomics – the impact of omnipotent neoliberal politico-economic superstructures and far-right ideology on domestic grassroots existence.

These are themes epitomised in the narratives of *Winter's Bone* (Debra Granik, 2010), *Red State* (Kevin Smith, 2011), *Compliance* (Craig Zobel, 2012), *The East* (Zal Batmanglij, 2013), *Night Moves* (Kelly Reichardt, 2013) and *The Peanut Butter Falcon* (Tyler Nilson and Michael Schwartz, 2019). This commonality of socio-political thematic content shared by some contemporary new Indian and American independent films again reiterates and foregrounds the contemporary glocal ethos of the Indian Indies which delineates them from the previous Parallel cinema movement. This facet also underscores the new wave of Indian Indies' simultaneous exogenous and endogenous entanglements with an Indian socio-political milieu of concomitant globalisation and localisation.

It is important to bear in mind that the new Indies are largely the products of a younger generation of Indian filmmakers, who have honed their filmmaking craft in the digital age – Shubhashish Bhutiani was 26 years old when he directed *Mukti Bhawan/Hotel Salvation* (2016), and Chaitanya Tamhane was 28 when he made *Court* (2014). The new wave Indie films are conceived in the crucible of globalisation and digital streaming platforms. By that token, they are immersed in an entirely different socio-economic, cultural, political and cinematic landscape from their Parallel cinema predecessors. Eventually, the death knell of the Parallel cinema movement was sounded in the 1980s by the rejection of these arthouse films as 'elitist' by general audiences in favour of the mainstream commercial entertainment-based Hindi films emerging en masse from the Bombay (Mumbai) film industry – which in the early '90s came to be christened, rather controversially, as Bollywood.

Diverging from the recondite exclusivity of Parallel cinema, the new Indian Indies stand apart in their assiduous attempts to gain wider audiences through enhanced local, national and global visibility often through digital platforms such as Netflix and Amazon Prime Video. Audience perceptions in contemporary India have also undergone a paradigm shift, particularly urban viewers who are more willing to engage with a broader spectrum of Indian films. Widening avenues of access via satellite television channels, video-on-demand web streaming portals and BitTorrent downloads have magnified not only film access but audience awareness, leading towards a more pluralistic and inclusive attitude to the new Indies that may not have been afforded their more arcane and niche Parallel cinema cousins.

Hinglish films

Apart from Parallel cinema, the new Indies' shared kinship with another notable yet less illustrious and largely overlooked niche set of urban films that emerged concurrent with India's liberalisation in the early '90s – Hinglish films. The portmanteau word Hinglish indicates films that juxtapose Hindi and English dialogues – code-switching between and code-mixing the two languages seamlessly as reflected in the daily practice of Indians in urban centres such as Mumbai, Bangalore, New Delhi, Kolkata, Chennai and Hyderabad. The Hinglish films were sporadic in terms of output with a paltry number of shoestring budget films released often through painstaking self-funded efforts of debutant directors. Examples include *English August* (Dev Benegal, 1994), *Split Wide Open* (Dev Benegal, 1999), *Everybody Says I'm Fine* (Rahul Bose, 2002), *Bombay Boys* (Kaizad Gustad, 1998) and *Hyderabad Blues* (Nagesh Kukunoor, 1998) which dealt with urban-centric Indian issues against the backdrop of India's liberalisation in the '90s. The Hinglish films of the 1990s and 2000s showed some characteristics of contemporary new Indian Indie cinema.

Importantly, in relation to tracing the evolutionary trajectory of the new Indies, the Hinglish films distinguished themselves from Bollywood by framing alternative storylines that dealt openly with sexuality, social and political problems, moral dilemmas and gender issues from a particularly cosmopolitan and liberal progressive outlook that circumvented Bollywood's traditional romantic song and dance preoccupation. For instance, Nagesh Kukunoor's Hinglish school boarding coming-of-age story *Rockford* (1999) could be situated as a touchstone for Vandana Kataria's more incisive and visceral new independent film *Noblemen* (2018) which delves into repressed homosexuality and violent bullying in an elite north Indian boarding school.

In this context, *Mr. and Mrs. Iyer* (2002), *Being Cyrus* (2005), *Life in a Metro* (2007) and *Honeymoon Travels Pvt Ltd.* (2007) featured not only the bilingual Hindi-English dialogue characteristic of the eponymous Hinglish category, but exhibited early manifestations of hybridity of form, style and content that would later characterise the new wave of Indies from 2010. These films also featured a motley assortment of Bollywood stars and art-house film actors, attempting to blend unconventional urban-centric content with more mainstream elements of romance and comedy.

Crucially, the low-budget Hinglish films from the 1990s to the early 2000s were never truly able to cohere into a genuinely cohesive corpus or genre of alternative films through consistent or prolific production output nor were they able to gain a dedicated local, national or global audience and wider exhibition platform.

Vernacular regional cinema

Akin to its diverse cinematic forms, India is a fissiparous country of 28 states and eight union territories, comprising 22 languages and innumerable dialects. Regional or vernacular films are terms used to refer to both the mainstream and alternative sectors of language-specific film industries in corresponding Indian states. As mentioned, the southern Indian states of Tamil Nadu, Kerala, Andhra Pradesh, Telangana and Karnataka all have their own thriving film industries distinct from the Mumbai-based Hindi film leviathan of Bollywood. Maharashtra, the state of which Mumbai is the capital, has a rich tradition of arthouse cinema – bespoke films made in the indigenous language, Marathi.

Identifying the distinction between the new wave of Indian Indies and the vernacular arthouse low-budget independent films corresponding to each specific Indian state may appear confusing. By and large, independent vernacular or regional language films that gain a wider national and international audience through critical acclaim, exposure at film festivals, enhanced levels of publicity and magnified channels of exhibition and distribution are often co-opted into the new wave of Indian Indie films. These films often possess form, style and content that allow them to render specifically local-level storylines and thematic matter universally palatable or generally accessible to audiences across boundaries of culture, nation and language.

Independent films in regional languages that remain locked within the boundaries of their state in relation to production, exhibition and distribution generating only localised visibility, accessibility, economic and cultural impact are regarded as regional or vernacular films. This tenuous but important distinction between widely visible Indies and local or regional-level alternative vernacular films therefore demonstrates the fluidity of the category 'Indie' in the Indian context. Broadly speaking, a limited number of vernacular independent films gain the national and international visibility that initiates them into the new wave of Indian Indies. To illustrate, an obscure small-budget martial arts comedy film from a remote part of Assam *Local Kung Fu* (2013) made on a budget of £1000 joined the ranks of the new Indies through box-office success and nationwide and even international exhibition.

IT programmer turned filmmaker Pawan Kumar's sophomore film – *Lucia* (2013), a low-budget crowdfunded Kannada film – blossomed into an unprecedented box-office hit, not only in Kumar's home state Karnataka, but across multiplexes in India and around the international film festival circuit. The success of this local film enabled Kumar to sell the multilingual remake rights to Fox Studios.

Similarly, another independently funded Kannada film *Thithi*, set in rural Karnataka and featuring local villagers as actors, became an unlikely international film festival success story. This wider access and recognition differentiates regional vernacular language films considered part of the independent Indian new wave from their counterparts that remain restricted to exhibition within state boundaries. Overall, these nuances underscore the stratifications, gradations, mutations and variations that comprise the conceptual basis of what 'independent' means in relation to the new wave of Indian Indies.

References

Appadurai, A. (1990). Disjuncture and difference in the global economy. *Public Culture*, 2(2), pp. 1–24.

Bhambra, P. (2017). *The fine line between Bollywood and independent Indian cinema*. ATA: Award Winning Video Production Company in London. [online] Available at: www.arttouchesart.com/the-fine-line-between-bollywood-and-independent-indian-cinema [Accessed 29 Dec. 2020].

Castells, M. (1996). *The rise of the network society*. Oxford: Blackwell.

Dasgupta, A. and Sethumadhavan, S. (2014). *The Other Way*. [online] Youtube.com. Available at: https://www.youtube.com/watch?v=T2a05JeF47Y [Accessed 28 December 2021].

Dasgupta, P. (2012). The Indie picture: Cinema beyond Bollywood – Times of India. *The Times of India*. [online] Available at: https://timesofindia.indiatimes.com/entertainment/hindi/bollywood/news/The-Indie-Picture-Cinema-beyond-Bollywood/articleshow/16251250.cms [Accessed 29 June 2020].

Devasundaram, A. (2014). Cyber buccaneers, public and pirate spheres: The phenomenon of BitTorrent downloads in the transforming terrain of Indian cinema. *Media International Australia*, 152, pp. 108–118.

Devasundaram, A. (2016). *India's new independent cinema: Rise of the hybrid*. New York: Routledge.

Devasundaram, A. (2018). *Indian Cinema Beyond Bollywood: The New Independent Cinema Revolution*. New York: Routledge.

Devasundaram, A. (2021). Tracing Bergman in contemporary Indian cinema: Philosophical cross-connections in *through a glass darkly*, *ship of Theseus* and *dear molly*. In: H. Ford and D. Humphrey, eds., *Bergman world: Perspectives on the iconic Swedish filmmaker's work*, *popular communication*, pp. 1–16.

Devasundaram, A. (2021). Tracing Bergman in Contemporary Indian Cinema: Philosophical Cross-Connections in Through a Glass Darkly, Ship of Theseus and Dear Molly. In: H. Ford and D. Humphrey, eds., *Bergman World, Popular Communication, The International Journal of Media and Culture*, 19(2), 96–111. DOI: 10.1080/15405702.2020.1868046

Devasundaram, A. (forthcoming in 2022). Local realism, Indian independent film as a socio-political medium. In: A. Taha and D. Menon, eds., *Cinemas of the global south: Towards a new aesthetics*. New York: Routledge.

Dwyer, R. (2011). *Zara Hatke!* The new middle classes and the segmentation of Hindi cinema. In: H. Donner, ed., *A way of life: Being middle-class in contemporary India*. Oxon: Routledge, pp. 184–208.

Film Companion. (2021). *Dibakar Banerjee on what independent cinema means.* [online] Available at: www.facebook.com/watch/?v=977842059717286 [Accessed 28 Aug. 2021].

Gehlawat, A. (2015). *Twenty-first century Bollywood.* Oxon: Routledge.

Ghosh, S. (2017). A new breed of film composers. *mint.* [online] Available at: www. livemint.com/Leisure/EmFqUsN1XRijcBPPKFnajP/A-new-breed-of-original-film-composers.html [Accessed 28 Aug. 2021].

Gopal, S. (2011). *Conjugations: Marriage and form in new Bollywood cinema.* Chicago: The University of Chicago Press.

Guneratne, A.R. (2003). Introduction. In: A.R. Guneratne and W. Dissanayake, eds., *Rethinking third cinema.* New York: Routledge, pp. 1–28.

IIF. (2021). Welcome to IIF. *India Independent Films.* [online] Available at: https:// indiaindependentfilms.com/ [Accessed 29 Aug. 2021].

Kavitha, S. (2020). In streaming services era, indie film-makers star in the new normal. *Fridaymagazine.ae.* [online] Available at: https://fridaymagazine.ae/life-culture/people-profiles/in-streaming-services-era-indie-film-makers-star-in-the-new-normal-1.2309146 [Accessed 3 May 2021].

Mazierska, E. and Rascaroli, L. (2003). *From Moscow to Madrid: Postmodern cities, European cinema.* London: I. B. Tauris & Co Ltd.

Mazumdar, R. (2010). Friction, collision and the grotesque: The dystopic fragments of Bombay cinema. In: G. Prakash, ed., *Noir urbanisms: Dystopic images of the modern city.* Princeton, NJ: Princeton University Press, pp. 150–186.

Narine, N. (2010). Global trauma and the cinematic network society. *Critical Studies in Media Communication*, 27(3), 209–234.

Rai, A. (2019). *Jugaad time ecologies of everyday hacking in India.* London: Duke University Press.

Rawle, S. (2018). *Transnational cinema: An introduction.* London: Palgrave.

Raindance.org. (2015). Indian indie films vs Bollywood. *Raindance.* [online] Available at: https://raindance.org/indian-indie-films-vs-bollywood/ [Accessed 29 Aug. 2021].

Sakula, D. (2015). Indian indie films Vs Bollywood – Raindance. *Raindance.org.* [online] Available at: www.raindance.org/indian-indie-films-vs-bollywood/ [Accessed 29 Dec. 2020].

Singh, S. (2021). Why Neeraj Ghaywan's short Geeli Pucchi is a must-watch. *India Today.* [online] Available at: www.indiatoday.in/india-today-insight/story/why-neeraj-ghaywan-s-short-geeli-pucchi-is-a-must-watch-1791405-2021-04-15?fbc lid=IwAR0O56-y8PpmVuCBzJbzaBqy72s5IhCGb7ixmYENf6e3J8DJqBqw FCm5_R90 [Accessed 6 May 2021].

Verma, R. (2011). Beyond Bollywood: Indian cinema's new cutting edge. *The Guardian.* [online] Available at: www.theguardian.com/film/2011/jun/23/india-independent-cinema [Accessed 29 Aug. 2021].

2 Breaking Bollywood's bastion

Radical, refreshing and revolutionary stories

Overview

This chapter delineates distinct ways in which new Indian Indies differ from Bollywood through divergent thematic content. It will cover salient points relating to Indie films' critical and topical engagement with a broad spectrum of discourses including LGBTQ+ and female-centric perspectives, political power structures and caste-based discrimination. Overall, this chapter emphasises how a distinctly divergent and interrogative interpretation of often taboo and controversial content from the perspectives of ordinary, marginalised and powerless protagonists demarcates the Indies as an alternative to Bollywood. The topical and unconventional themes and issues broached by the new Indies are in conversation with daily discourses and current affairs in India, intertwining local, national and global levels.

Breaking the Bollywood barrier of film representation

Since their rise to visibility in 2010, the Indies have been pitted in an uneven David versus Goliath struggle with Bollywood. Despite producing only around one-third of the total Indian film output (Rawle, 2018, p. 28), the Mumbai-based Bollywood industry dominates the Indian cultural landscape and popular consciousness through box-office revenue generation, monopolisation of funding, exhibition and distribution channels, an idolised star system and the industry's ideological posturing as a unifying 'national cinema' (see section on meta-hegemony in Chapter 4).

Bollywood's status as the pre-eminent form of popular culture in India is transposable globally, where 'Bollywood' has become a synonymous term for all things Indian. However, within India's national borders and amongst non-resident Indian diaspora in western nations, Bollywood's dominance resides in its role as sanctifier and defender of 'Indian' traditions, morals, customs, values, religious rituals and nationalism alongside serving as a

DOI: 10.4324/9781003089001-3

fountainhead of escapist song and dance-based glitzy mass entertainment. Bollywood seamlessly slips into this double narrative of modern India, adorning the garb of national cultural custodian whilst propagating the idea of new neoliberal India – a consumer society unequivocally open to multinational corporate investment. This ideological duality aligns perfectly with the ruling right-wing Hindu fundamentalist BJP government's own strategy of neutralising India's constitutional secular democratic credentials in order to establish a majoritarian theocratic Hindu *rashtra* (nation) whilst simultaneously cementing an elite class of entrepreneurial oligarchs whose financial empires provide economic sustenance to the regime's religious and political masterplan.

Bollywood's commercial Hindi cinema has consistently been peddled to the Indian public as 'wholesome family entertainment'. This is notwithstanding sexually suggestive and misogynistic song and dance sequences, privileging of majority Hindu ideology as the default 'national identity', patriarchy, gendered roles and gratuitous violence in the avatar of action films. The purported universality of Bollywood as 'films for all the family to enjoy' has entailed that taboo subject matter beyond the boundaries of what is deemed socially, culturally, politically and religiously acceptable is largely swept under the carpet by the mainstream film industry. To a degree, commercial Hindi cinema in the 1970s and '80s, before the 'Bollywood' boom in the 1990s, did grapple with themes of social injustice, wealth disparity and state corruption, especially in the popular 'angry young man' working-class hero films featuring Amitabh Bachchan. However, with India's free market liberalisation in the 1990s, commercial Hindi cinema in its Bollywood avatar promoted a vision of upper-class affluence, globetrotting and sybaritic lifestyles, courting Indian diasporic interest and espousing a Hindu nationalist Indian identity.

The #MeTooIndia movement in 2018 revealed routinised sexual abuse, a 'casting couch' culture, entrenched misogynistic attitudes, standards and practices in the Bollywood industry (Devasundaram, 2020a). The industry's structural issues with sexism are indexical of Bollywood's enduringly gendered and patriarchal onscreen representation. On this level, the most problematic trope in Bollywood blockbusters is the 'item number' – a stand-alone sexualised song and dance sequence usually incepted indiscriminately into the narrative with little or no connection to the film plot. The item number features an 'item girl' – an erotic siren or seductress whose sole purpose is the visual titillation of the male hero, and by proxy, arousal of the scopophilic desires of the film's male audience.

The item number has become a normalised and indeed essential feature of Bollywood songs. Often, item songs are released prior to their corresponding films and have often helped make or break films at the box-office.

The uncontested adoption and celebration of item numbers as part of pan-Indian culture speaks to the ideological pulling power of Bollywood as a monolithic marker of national and global Indian diasporic identity. Similarly, the question of homosexual desire, contentious in Indian culture and society, has largely been airbrushed, bowdlerised, belittled or erased from mainstream Hindi and Bollywood cinema.

It must be noted that the new Indies are often intersectional in their conjoining of discourses relating to women's issues, LGBTQ+ rights, caste discrimination, politics and domestic familial situations. Notable examples include *Peepli Live* (Anusha Rizvi, 2010), *I Am* (Onir, 2010), *Papilio Buddha, Ka Bodyscapes* (Jayan Cherian, 2013, 2016), *Angry Indian Goddesses* (Pan Nalin, 2015), *Sairat/Wild* (Nagraj Manjule, 2016), *Court* (Chaitanya Tamhane, 2014), *Haider* (Vishal Bhardwaj, 2014), *Aligarh* (Hansal Mehta, 2016), *Unfreedom* (Raj Amit Kumar, 2015)*, Lipstick Under My Burkha* (Alankrita Shrivastava, 2016), *Ajji* (Devashish Makhija, 2017), *Masaan* (Neeraj Ghaywan, 2015), *K.D./Karuppudurai* (Madhumita, 2019), *Life of an Outcast* (Pawan Shrivastava, 2018), *The Great Indian Kitchen* (Jeo Baby, 2021) *and Geeli Pucchi/Ajeeb Daastaans* (Neeraj Ghaywan et al., 2021). Several overlapping strands are woven into the tapestry of these and several other Indie films. This ability of the Indies to generate multiple intersecting lines of analysis, debate and discourse renders them a transdiscursive contemporary Indian film form. The next sections offer specific insights into the spectrum of themes that distinguish Indies from Bollywood.

LGBTQ+ liberation

Setting the context

In a landmark ruling on 6 September 2018, the Indian Supreme Court abolished Section 377 – a British colonial law imposed in 1860 criminalising homosexuality between consenting adults. The abrogation of this outdated and discriminatory law marked a transformative and euphoric moment in the longstanding battle for LGBTQ+ rights in India. It is important to acknowledge the role of new Indian Indies that have contributed significantly to foregrounding and championing LGBTQ+ stories and themes that were largely ignored, ridiculed or overlooked by mainstream Hindi cinema. Bollywood films and their forebears – commercial Hindi Cinema – have traditionally adopted crude, disparaging and essentialising representations of LGBTQ+ characters, often reducing them to stereotypes, caricatures and objects of comedy, mockery and debasement (Kaur, 2017, p. 27). Depictions of homosocial 'bromances' couched as 'yaarana' or bonding between straight male stars have been a consistent trope spanning commercial

Hindi cinema and Bollywood – from iconic commercial Hindi film *Sholay* (1975) to *Dostana* (2008). This soft-pedalled approach of dancing around the urgent and central issue of affirming LGBTQ+ identities as a legitimate mode of selfhood and social being has hindered more than helped the LGBTQ+ community seeking fair and diverse representation in Indian cinema (Kaur, 2017, pp. 26–28).

In general, Bollywood's unwillingness to come out and confront directly the skeletons in India's socio-cultural closet stems from Bollywood's self-adopted role as cultural custodian of an imagined national narrative of traditional 'Indian morals and values'. Bollywood's enduring provision of patriarchal and heteronormative 'wholesome family entertainment' has rendered it incumbent on alternative filmmaking sectors in Indian cinema to represent sexual minorities with more nuance, substance and depth.

Expression of queer onscreen identities could be traced back to *Badnam Basti* (Prem Kapoor, 1971) – the first Indian film to represent a homosexual relationship. Hitherto considered lost, the film was rediscovered serendipitously in a Berlin film archive in 2020 in the midst of the global Covid-19 pandemic. *Badnam Basti* is significant, considering it was released during the early days of the new wave of Parallel cinema (Ghosh, 2020) amongst seminal films such as *Uski Roti, Bhuvan Shome* and *Sara Akash*.

It is also important to affirm the crucial role played by Canadian-Indian crossover filmmaker Deepa Mehta's controversial film *Fire*. On its release in 1996, the film raised the hackles of right-wing Hindu fundamentalist groups and conservative sections of Indian society. Vigilante extremist Hindu militias vandalised cinema halls screening the film. The pathbreaking portrayal by Indian screen icon Shabana Azmi and Nandita Das of sisters-in-law trapped in loveless heterosexual marriages finding love and solace in each other set a precedent for unrelenting film representation that challenged dominant religious, political, social and cultural norms.

Between 1996 and the early 2000s, a sporadic handful of urban Hinglish films such as the short film anthology *Bomgay* (1996), Kaizad Gustad's *Bombay Boys* (1998) and Mahesh Dattani's *Mango Souffle* (2002) endeavoured to portray sexual minorities. Pioneering gay activist and filmmaker Sridhar Rangayan through his independent production company Solaris Pictures sought consistently to challenge the social status quo that stigmatised and suppressed free articulation of LGBTQ+ sexuality. Rangayan's films including *Gulabi Aina/The Pink Mirror* and *Yours Emotionally* were conceived from shoestring budgets and were hampered by censorship and restricted avenues of exhibition and distribution. Openly gay filmmaker Onir's *My Brother Nikhil* (2005) was another milestone in the journey towards accentuated visibility of LGBTQ+ lived experience onscreen.

From 2010 to the eventual decriminalisation of homosexuality in 2018, the vociferously radical call for India to reorientate its attitude to LGBTQ+ identities has emerged cinematically from new wave Indian Indies. In a socio-cultural milieu skewed towards religious adherence, patriarchal attitudes and heteronormative family structures, new Indian Indie films have served as a strident platform and a vital emancipatory space for cinematic articulation of LGBTQ+ narratives. The Indies' role in raising awareness and assisting the campaign to overturn Section 377 is epitomised in the promotional strapline #ComeOutandQuestion that accompanied Hansal Mehta's *Aligarh* (2016). This visibility was all the more important during the intervening period of uncertainty, vacillation and indecision between 2013 – when Section 377, repealed in 2009, was reinstated – and 2018 when the law was annulled.

Films from 2010 to 2021

Onir's crowdfunded anthology film *I Am* punctuated 2010 with the film's fourth story instalment *I Am Omar* focusing on the brutalisation of a young gay man by a police officer (see Chapter 6). This theme was inspired by myriad actual experiences of LGBTQ+ people across India, who had been victims of extortion, assault and incarceration by agents of law enforcement. Featuring Rahul Bose, one of the pioneering actors in Hinglish films of the 1990s and 2000s, the film also publicised its portrayal of India's 'first onscreen gay love scene'.

Made on a minimal budget, the Gujarati film *Meghadhanushya/The Colour of Life* (2013), directed by K R Devmani, features the disinherited royal scion Prince Manvendra Singh Gohil whose narration informs the film's attempt to destigmatise homosexuality. Jayan Cherian's brace of controversial Malayalam films *Papilio Buddha* in 2013 and *Ka Bodyscapes* in 2016 offer searing portrayals of queer themes that intersect with grassroots narratives of caste and gender-based oppression, homophobia and religious orthodoxy. The Revising Committee of the Central Board for Film Certification (CBFC) withheld a release certificate for *Ka Bodyscapes*, accusing the film of 'ridiculing, insulting and humiliating Hindu religion', portraying 'Hindu God Hanuman in books titled I am Gay' and depicting female masturbation (Anandan, 2016). These scenarios demonstrate how critical and self-evaluative content in independent Indian films are often antithetical to the anodyne and fantastical themes in Bollywood films.

Raj Amit Kumar's polemical *Unfreedom* was banned by the CBFC, and the director's petition to the Film Certification Appellate Tribunal (FCAT) was also negated and the injunction upheld. This action, reminiscent of the reinstatement of Section 377 by the supreme court ruling in 2013, demonstrated how legal and juridical power structures are also invoked to control and debilitate LGBTQ+ expression from the arts and culture sector. The film's dual narrative portrays a forbidden lesbian relationship alongside parallel reflection on the splintering social effects of extreme religious fundamentalism in Islam, thereby providing a concomitant insight into doctrinaire and dogmatic aspects of both Hinduism and Islam. In a graphic sequence, the father of one of the women involved in the lesbian love affair gives his consent to a group of policemen to rape his daughter in a jail cell to 'cure' her of her 'sickness', as he witnesses the act. The film was banned in India and this catchphrase used as a selling point – a reverse strategy often utilised by Indie filmmakers to augment visibility and distribution. *Unfreedom* by dint of its very moniker confronts the compromised, contradictory and contaminated form of democracy in contemporary India, where the conceptual idea of democracy is distinctly dislocated from its daily performance.

In clearing a pathway towards highlighting and normalising LGBTQ+ narratives, *Dear Dad* (Tanuj Bhramar, 2016) starring Tamil film actor Arvind Swamy utilises a father-son road trip premise to enact the role reversal scenario of a middle-aged father coming out to his young teenage son. Sudhanshu Saria's idiosyncratically titled *Loev* charts the cosmopolitan existence and romantic involvement of two young men and was screened at the 2016 BFI Flare Festival in London. *Loev* marked a significant step towards representing and legitimising ordinary everyday experiences of gay people (see Chapter 6). The film refrained from reproducing stereotypes of gay characters as victims whose lives invariably result in tragic conclusions. This representational shift of direction even within the Indie terrain was distinctive, considering the more visceral and violent narrations of traumatic events in *I Am*, *Unfreedom* and *Aligarh*. Based on true-life incidents surrounding a tabloid news media crew invading the home of Prof. Shrinivas Siras of Aligarh University and filming him having sex with a Muslim rickshaw puller, *Aligarh* was a watershed Indie film in 2016.

Sridhar Rangayan's *Evening Shadows* (2018) charts a young professional photographer Kartik's (Devansh Doshi) coming out to his ultra-orthodox traditional Brahmin family in small town South India. The narrative is set during the 2013 supreme court verdict recriminalising homosexuality, rendering the film's local realist aesthetics and son's defiant declaration of his sexuality to his misogynistic and homophobic Brahmin father a microcosmic local-level interrogation of a larger national discourse.

Normalisation of same-sex love through naturalistic portrayals in diverse regions of India is notable in Indie films such as *Parched* (2016) set in the arid rural region of Rajasthan. In one sequence, Lajjo (Radhika Apte), serially abused by her violent alcoholic husband, flees to her friend Rani

(Tannishtha Chatterjee) in the aftermath of a particularly brutal assault. As Rani ministers gently to Lajjo's bruises, her compassion for her best friend crystallises into a moment of deep tenderness and spontaneous human bonding. This sequence featuring two prominent standard bearers of new Indian Indie cinema typifies the Indies' broader boundary-pushing facets in terms of normalising LGBTQ+ relationships on screen.

Female same-sex intimacy, bonding, solidarity and desire are also foregrounded in several other independent Indian films such as *Margarita With a Straw* (Shonali Bose, 2014) starring Kalki Koechlin, another recognised actor from the Indie space. The film embraces twin themes of disability and lesbian desire blending these topics through a local meets global perspective. Set in a remote coastal village in Tamil Nadu, *Kattumaram/Catamaran* (Swarnavel Eswaran, 2018) shines a light on conservative local customs, traditions, and social and cultural mores that privilege heterosexual marriage as the inevitable fate of young women in the rural space. Intersectional aspects of gender and sexual identity specific to India form the backdrop of Dalit filmmaker Neeraj Ghaywan's story instalment *Geeli Pucchi/Sloppy Kisses* in the Netflix anthology film *Ajeeb Daastaans* (2021).

In terms of transgender representation, Bollywood continues its 'long history of both mocking and vilifying trans people in a way that could have dangerous real-life implications' as exemplified by big-budget comedy-horror film *Laxmii* (2020) which portrays its trans character as predatory and an incarnation of 'supernatural evil' (Jha and Holland, 2020). There have been a growing number of independent films focusing on serious and substantive transgender storylines and characters. Films such as *Ek Aasha* (2018) with a non-professional transgender cast, Assamese film *Fireflies* (2019) and Kannada-language *Naan Avanalla, Avalu/I Am Not He, I am She* (2015) reflect the regional and linguistic diversity of independent Indian films raising the visibility of transgender lived experience. Anup Singh's *Qissa: The Tale of a Lonely Ghost* (2013) introduces a transgendering gaze in the film's historical narrative about a Sikh family's traumatic experience of the India-Pakistan Partition in 1947. The family patriarch Umber Singh's (Irrfan Khan) obsession to have a male child causes him to impose a masculine identity on his daughter, Kanwar (Tilottama Shome).

As mentioned in the first chapter, the alternative thematic orientation and hybrid formal and stylistic sensibilities of Indian Indie films have served as the template for expanded web series on online streaming platforms. Amazon Prime Video series *Paatal Lok/Netherworld* (2020) features a transgender character played by trans female actor Mairembam Ronaldo Singh from the North Eastern Indian state of Manipur. A transgender character (although played by cis female actor Kubbra Sait) plays a prominent and nuanced role in *Sacred Games* (2018) – India's first original Netflix web series, investigating intersections between police violence, political power, underworld mafia and religious majoritarian ideology. Tamil language Indian films *Super Deluxe* (2019) and *Peranbu* (2019) which co-stars trans female actor Anjali Ameer also present positive depictions of transgender women whose resilience and tenacity contribute to ultimate social acceptance of their gender identity. The intersectional aspects of the preceding films and web series are embedded in their exploration of policing, politics, class, caste, religion, gender and sexuality.

As described in this section, the mainstreaming of LGBTQ+ stories and protagonists signifies the new Indies' role in instigating a gradual but profound metamorphosis not only in mainstream Bollywood but also Indian socio-cultural attitudes towards sexual minorities. With their sustained and wide-ranging representation of the spectrum of queer identities, Indian Indies must be accorded due credit for assisting the process of radically reconstructing LGBTQ+ representation in the contemporary Indian cinema terrain.

F-Rated films

In terms of film representation, Bollywood is often culpable of banalising and belittling women, consigning them to sex-objects in song and dance set-pieces called 'item numbers':

> [in Bollywood] the female protagonist is often depicted as the beautiful love interest of the hero. Such representations in Indian cinema have resulted in relegating female characters to passive/insignificant roles that demand beauty labour instead of holistic dispositions of them.
>
> (Chatterjee and Rastogi, 2020, p. 272)

By contrast, the Indies are a bastion for strong female roles both behind and in front of the camera (Devasundaram, 2020a) (also see Chapter 4). Several of the new wave Indie films fulfil the criteria of the F-Rating – a template conceived in 2014 by Holly Tarquini, creative director of the Bath Film Festival. The F-Rating relates to female-centric films that are directed, written and performed by women (Devasundaram, 2020a).

Since 2010, the Indie sector has served as a springboard for several emerging and first-time filmmakers. Anusha Rizvi's *Peepli Live* and Kiran Rao's *Dhobi Ghat* are two pathbreaking films from 2010 that set a precedent for the new wave to follow. Since then, a plethora of films about female empowerment and feminist agency foregrounding female characters include Leena Yadav's *Parched*, India's first all-female 'buddy' road movie *Angry Indian Goddesses*, Geetu Mohandas's *Liar's Dice*, Anjali

Menon's *Bangalore Days*, Ruchika Oberoi's *Island City* and Akriti Singh's *Toofan Mail*. These offbeat non-mainstream films signpost the revolutionising amplification of female voices and enhanced representation of women spearheaded by the new Indian Indie film sector.

Angry Indian Goddesses about seven women who congregate for a bohemian weekend features an ensemble of recognisable independent actors. The film confronts the malaises of rape, sexual abuse and gender inequality in Indian society. Its bold portrayal of a lesbian couple who decide to get married in a church in Goa speaks unflinchingly to the prevailing status quo and social order. The film's entwining narrative strands of lesbian love, class disparities, female subjectivities and patriarchal power are reflective of the discursive intersectionality of several new Indies.

Demonstrating diversity of film form and style, *Liar's Dice* (2013), written and directed by Geetu Mohandas and starring Geetanjali Thapa, was India's entry to the foreign language section of the Oscars whilst writer-director-editor Gitanjali Rao specialises in the animation film format, rendering realist narratives including *Bombay Rose* (2019). *Parched*, scripted and directed by Leena Yadav (see Chapter 6), is another example of an F-Rated Indie film that generated considerable impact with its radical narrative of four rural women throwing off the shackles of patriarchal oppression in a break to freedom. By exposing the troubling and exploitative dimensions of the Bollywood item number, this Indie film interrogates the larger patriarchal cultural codes linking the item number with gender-based violence (Devasundaram and Barn, 2020b).

Anarkali of Arrah (Avinash Das, 2017) is another independent film that harnesses the Bollywood item number trope meta-referentially to unveil entrenched sexism and normalised patriarchy. Set in the provincial hinterlands of Bihar, India's poorest state, the film focuses on Anarkali, a Muslim *nautch* girl whose profession is performing bawdy and prurient song and dance for largely male audiences in rustic Arrah. Anarkali draws the line between creative expression and sexual consent when she rejects the sexual overtures of a powerful university vice-chancellor with connections to the state chief minister. This draws her into a disproportionate battle with political forces, police and Arrah's residents. In the film's affirmative narrative, toxic masculinity is combated successfully by Anarkali who reclaims agency over her body and declares that consent is non-negotiable.

Formal experimentation as a capsule to narrate feminist agency is exemplified by supernatural thriller *Bulbbul* (2020), written and directed by Anvita Dutt. The film's visualisation of aristocratic landed gentry in 19th century Bengal through period-specific mise-en-scene and ornate production design evokes comparisons with Satyajit Ray's iconic domestic dramas *Charulata* (1964) and *Ghare-Baire* (1984). Co-produced by

Bollywood star Anushka Sharma, *Bulbbul* epitomises the Indies' strong female-centric focus but also reiterates their hybridity in terms of strategic alliances with the mainstream film industry. The Indie space also provides a platform for debut female filmmakers such as Akriti Singh who wrote, directed and starred in *Toofan Mail* whilst scriptwriter Rohena Gera directed and co-produced her first feature *Sir* (2018). A preponderantly female production team collaborated to create Anu Menon's *Waiting* (2015). Alankrita Shrivastava's *Lipstick Under My Burkha* is arguably one of the most impactful and polemical feminist new independent Indian films, generating debate and controversy owing to the initial injunction on the film's release due to censorship authorities deeming the film too 'lady oriented' (see Chapter 3).

The new wave of female-rated independent Indian films is accompanied by the burgeoning prominence of female cinematographers, editors and sound designers. Editors such as Aarti Bajaj, Deepa Bhatia and Namrata Rao have helmed editing on several independent film projects. The Indian Women Cinematographers Collective (IWCC), established in 2017 and composed of accomplished directors of photography – Fowzia Fatima, Anjuli Shukla, Deepti Gupta, Savita Singh inter alia – published the first online directory of female technicians in 2019 (IWCC, 2021).

Political polemic

Indie entanglement in an Indian socio-political matrix

As mentioned in the previous chapter, India's ascendant new wave of independent Indies are a self-reflexive, distinctly *glocal* cohort of contemporary Indian cinema – global in aesthetic attributes but local in thematic content. The Indies' focus on ordinary everyday ground-level stories often open a window for these films to place India's secular and democratic constitutional credentials in a politically interrogative spotlight.

Consecutive election victories gained by the BJP in 2014 and 2019 have ushered India into an era of right-wing Hindu majoritarian nationalism, spearheaded by the populist approach of Prime Minister Narendra Modi. The BJP is the political branch of the Hindu *Sangh* family tree of organisations under the ideological masthead of proto-fascist organisation the Rashtriya Swayamsevak Sangh (RSS), committed to converting India into a mono-religious Hindu *rashtra* (nation). As Christophe Jaffrelot (2021) notes in *Modi's India: Hindu Nationalism and the Rise of Ethnic Democracy*, this majoritarian agenda flies in the face of the Indian constitution which frames the country as a secular, democratic, socialist republic. With topical, often politically incisive storylines and alternative narratives, the

Indies act as disruptive dissenters and conscientious interjectors in Bollywood's dominant one-sided narration of the nation.

The new wave has spawned several seminal Indie films with discursive socio-political themes – 'state of the nation' stories inextricably intertwined with the state of entropy, volatility and vacillation that surrounds India's endangered democracy. BJP rule has been marked by state complicity and silence shrouding a spate of vigilante mob lynching and murder of minorities – particularly Muslims and Dalits – and routinised violence that accompanies the ruling government's rising brand of religious fascism.

Noteworthy political developments under the BJP banner include the controversial annulment in 2019 of Article 370, a constitutional law granting semi-autonomous special status to Jammu and Kashmir. Narendra Modi's government has also introduced a controversial Citizenship Amendment Act (CAA) and a National Register of Citizens (NRC) – strategic attempts to segregate and disenfranchise the nation's Muslim minority population. The state's endeavour to implement the CAA and NRC (see Chapter 3) proved controversial, sparking social unrest and mass protests across the nation. Students from leading left-liberal universities such as JNU in Delhi were at the vanguard of the civil society movement against the government's imposition of these discriminatory laws.

The BJP has also passed a parliament bill to corporatise the agriculture sector in India opening it out to indiscriminate foreign multinational investment thereby amplifying the precarious existence of indebted Indian farmers, reflected in a protracted pandemic of farmer suicides – the thematic locus for Anusha Rizvi's pathbreaking film *Peepli Live* in 2010. Registering their opposition to the BJP government's attempt to neoliberalise the farming sector, farmers from Punjab, Haryana and other northern states marched in protest, congregating in New Delhi on Republic Day in January 2021. In a politically strategic manoeuvre in November 2021, on the cusp of regional state elections, the Modi regime announced repeal of its proposed farming laws – a significant volte-face.

Several filmmakers and actors from the Indian Indie sector including Anurag Kashyap, Rahul Bose and Konkona Sen Sharma protested the Modi government's introduction of CAA and NRC. Several BJP politicians endeavoured to denounce Kashyap – an enduringly vocal critic of the Modi regime. BJP spokespersons and politicians attributed Kashyap's rejection of CAA and NRC to the filmmaker's disgruntlement with the BJP-led Uttar Pradesh state government's refusal to finance his ongoing film projects. Kashyap's BJP detractors alleged without substantiation that the previous chief minister of Uttar Pradesh, Akhilesh Yadav, had helped fund Kashyap's production of the Indie film *Masaan* (OutlookIndia.com, 2020). This scenario demonstrates the interconnections between politics and filmmaking outside the aesthetics of political representation on screen. In other words, politics from the local to the national level influence and inform multiple matrices of filmmaking in India – from Indies to Bollywood.

The following sections focus on some key political themes addressed by Indie films. It is important to add that in the Indian context, there is inevitable intermeshing and interplay between the socio-political discourses discussed under the following sub-headings.

The Kashmir question

The conflict-ridden Himalayan Kashmir region has long been a territorial bone of contention between India and Pakistan. Thematically, Kashmir has constituted a cinematic space of limbo when considering the potential for representative and nuanced cinematic investigations into the local lived experience of ordinary Kashmiri civilians caught in the crossfire between Indian security forces and militant separatists. Bollywood has often espoused bowdlerised, romanticised and jingoistic narratives whilst representing the region in action blockbusters such as *Mission Kashmir* (Vidhu Vinod Chopra, 2000), which often portray local Muslim Kashmiris as insurgent terrorists or naïve victims invariably susceptible to pro-Pakistan Islamic fundamentalist rhetoric. By contrast, Aamir Bashir's *Harud/Autumn* (2010), *Haider* (2014) directed by Vishal Bhardwaj, Rahat Kazmi's black comedy *Side A & Side B* (2017), documentarian Ashvin Kumar's fiction feature *No Fathers in Kashmir* and Aijaz Ahmed's *Hamid* (2019) have all formulated more textured and streamlined interpretations of Kashmiri politics from a kaleidoscope of locally specific filmic and contextual perspectives.

Harud adopts a minimalist 'slow cinema' approach to ponder on the inertia of existence in the Kashmir valley where access to mobile phones, the internet and cinema halls has been suspended in a form of 'digital apartheid' (JKCCS, 2020) from the rest of India. The film presents a ground-level glimpse into the stasis that surrounds civilian life in Kashmir which itself remains suspended in an interminable political conflict between India and Pakistan.

Whilst *Harud* meditates on the plight of Muslim Kashmiris' continual repression and subjugation by the settler colonialism of India's military and political apparatus (Osuri and Zia, 2020), one of the four story instalments in director Onir's portmanteau Indie film *I Am* (2010) seeks to provide perspectives of Muslim Kashmiris as well as the Hindu Kashmiri Pandit community who departed in a mass exodus from the valley following the intensifying political impasse and insurgent violence in the 1990s.

Haider (2014) is a film indigenisation of Shakespeare's *Hamlet* set in Kashmir and therefore brings to the fore the region's status as a perennial political flashpoint. *Hamid* (Aijaz Khan, 2018) is a more contemplative and even-handed evaluation of opposing sides of the violent Kashmir conflict, reminiscent of the representation of French occupation in *The Battle of Algiers* (Gillo Pontecorvo, 1966). *Hamid* is visualised through the naïve eyes of a fatherless 8-year-old Kashmiri Muslim boy charting his serendipitous connection with an Indian army soldier. Comparison could be drawn with similar Indies, notably, Ashvin Kumar's *No Fathers in Kashmir* (2019) which paints a nuanced portrait of turbulent daily local Kashmiri life that is nonetheless ensnared in a complex national and global discursive historical and political network.

In particular, *Haider, Harud* and *Hamid* interrogate an authoritarian Indian legislation – the Armed Forces Special Powers Act (AFSPA) – which gives Indian armed forces in politically sensitive areas such as Kashmir free rein to carry out search and arrest operations without a warrant and deploy firearms unilaterally. AFSPA has facilitated Indian security forces' enforced disappearances of innumerable Kashmiri civilians. These films also feature real life rallies by Kashmiri organisation Association of Parents of Disappeared Persons (APDP), blurring distinctions between fact and fiction, and in a politically explicit cinematic statement, demonstrating the link between AFSPA and the APDP.

Rahat Kazmi adopts an ostensibly softer approach of satirical comedy in *Side A & Side B* (2017), to convey the potent theme of a group of young Kashmiris trapped in political and cultural purgatory. In a region where cinema halls have all been shut down by the Indian state, the film's motley crew of characters resort to the farcical exercise of making their own film with meagre resources. This filmic figuration of dereliction, deprivation and stagnation synonymises the forged existences of Kashmiri civilians under the repressive rule of the Indian security apparatus. The aforementioned Indie films prefigure the concretisation of Indian settler colonialism in Kashmir – India's unilateral annexation of the state of Jammu and Kashmir (Osuri and Zia, 2020, pp. 251, 254) through abrogation of Article 370 in 2019. Therefore, the Indies present an alternative space to negotiate contentious political discourses surrounding the Kashmir question, which is often considered prohibited terrain in mainstream commercial films.

In summary, subjective interpretations of human rights and political conflict are mediated with verisimilitude, specificity and context in these Indie films. The aforementioned filmmakers are able to present multiple critical viewpoints without being beholden to sanctioning or privileging a dominant nationalistic discourse in the manner of Bollywood. Political cognisance and critical appraisal are facets that epitomise the Indies' positioning in an alternative space, where unlike Bollywood's obligatory regurgitation of the national narrative, Indies can engage with politically sensitive subject matter.

Challenging the caste system

Caste discrimination is an issue particular to India. The caste pyramid is largely based on a social 'tier system' conceived in ancient Hindu religious doctrine, spawning four principal social groups from 'high' to 'low' caste. At the top of the chain is the priestly Brahmin class, considered pure and elevated due to their exclusive custodianship of Hindu religious scriptures. Next in line is the Kshatriya or warrior land-owner class. The Vaishya or merchant class specialising in commerce and trade are positioned third in the tier. Bottom of the pile is the Shudra demographic, formerly known as 'untouchables' and now classified as Dalit or Scheduled Caste (SC). Dalits are often relegated to performing menial tasks which are deemed below the dignity and socio-religious status of the so-called 'higher' castes. In contemporary India, 'low-caste' Dalits are often consigned to occupations considered ritually unclean. These include 'manual scavenging', sweeping roads, collecting garbage, cleaning toilets and drains as represented in the Indie *Gutter Boy* (2021) or burning bodies at cremation pyres (ghats) as portrayed in *Masaan*. Another category – Adivasis or ethnic tribal groups classified officially as Scheduled Tribes (ST) akin to their Dalit counterparts – constitute a marginalised subaltern community at the lowest rung of the caste hierarchy.

Bollywood's majoritarian Hindu narrative is predicated largely on a *savarna* 'upper-caste' Brahmin vision of India (see Chapter 4 section on Dalit Studies) which is tellingly reflected in the dearth of mainstream commercial films with Dalit characters or themes. In an article on how 'Bollywood is selling Hindutva as history', Aditya Menon (2019) observes a 'subtext to the narrative of Hindu nationalism being pushed by Bollywood's new period dramas: supremacy of Brahmins and other Upper Castes like Rajputs and Marathas'. Big-budget blockbusters such as *Padmavat, Bajirao Mastani, Panipat: The Great Betrayal* and *Tanhaji: The Unsung Warrior* are deliberate distortions of Indian history designed to denigrate the Mughal period and position Muslim rulers as villainous foreign occupiers.

In this commercial cinema topography, Indie films have been a potent tool to challenge caste dynamics, entrenched social segregation and bigotry in contemporary Indian society and culture through a new wave of Dalit cinema. Several Indie films have taken on the taboo topic of caste-based discrimination, exposing the socio-political metanarratives that facilitate retrenchment and reproduction of this specifically Indian instantiation of ethnic bigotry. For instance, two trailblazing Marathi independent films,

Fandry/Pig (2013) and *Sairat/Wild* (2016) by director Nagraj Manjule, dig deep into the daily lived experience of the marginalised Dalit community exploring how inter-caste relationships are still stigmatised in modern India across the urban-rural divide. The films also expose how the discourse around caste is presided over by right-wing 'upper-caste' religious and political power structures.

Tamil film *Visaranai/Interrogation* (Vetrimaaran, 2016), India's entry to the foreign language section of the 89th Academy Awards, is a visceral portrayal of interstate divisions on the basis of caste, language and ethnic orientation. Five migrant Tamil workers in the neighbouring State of Andhra Pradesh find themselves incarcerated in a police station jail cell under false charges and are brutalised horrifically by the custodians of the law primarily because of their expendable subaltern status as Dalit migrant 'others' (Devasundaram, 2018a).

In this regard, vernacular Indie films correspond to their specific regional political constellations, exposing local nuances and textures that punctuate these political sub-domains. Films such as *Visaranai* also implicate political power structures in corruption, crimes and extra-judicial murders by emphasising the broader complicity between regional state governments and the centre. In this regard, the Indies demonstrate the concentric circles and capillary nature of power that – as mentioned earlier – make it essential to view Indian Indie film representations of politics and caste issues as a tapestry of interwoven discourses.

Resembling the portrayal in *Visaranai* of brutalised Dalit migrants, Jayan Cherian's *Papilio Buddha* about the victimisation of Dalits and expropriation of their land in Kerala was denied a certificate of release by the CBFC. This denial of exhibition demonstrates that the Indies' espousal of local narratives is often subordinated to national structures of political power and censorship (see Chapter 3).

Ajji/Grandmother (2017), Devashish Makhija's visceral and unorthodox rape-revenge story featuring veteran Marathi stage actor Sushama Deshpande, revolutionises the notion of social vigilantism by defying barriers of age, social class, caste and gender. The film's representation of an 'Avenging Ajji' engages with patriarchal political power, focusing on the eponymous elderly lady who transcends her slum dweller and 'lower-caste' status to single-handedly take on the brutal rapist who sexually assaulted her young granddaughter. The serial sex offender is portrayed as the son of an influential political leader of a Hindu ultra-right-wing fundamentalist party – a reference to the influence of the Hindu *Sangh* family of far-right political organisations specifically in Maharashtra state. The indictment in April 2018 of BJP politician Kuldeep Singh Sengar on the charge of raping a 17-year-old girl and the subsequent death of the victim's father in police custody in Uttar Pradesh (Seth, 2018) underpin the verisimilitude of *Ajji*'s premise whilst unveiling the nexus between politicians and the police in India. This fiction film's allusion to right-wing political power also draws comparisons with other Indie feature and documentary films that highlight the broader ascendancy of Hindu fundamentalist and xenophobic political ideology. Some examples include *Dhobi Ghat* (Kiran Rao, 2010), *The World Before Her* (Nisha Pahuja, 2012), *Court* (Chaitanya Tamhane, 2014), *Bhonsle* (Devashish Makhija, 2018) and *Garbage* (Q, 2018).

Article 15 is another of several independent films that reveal Indian constitutional principles that are routinely contravened and disregarded in daily practice. The film takes its title from constitutional Article 15 which forbids discrimination on the basis of caste, religion, race, sex or place of birth. Adopting the style of a police procedural, the film is loosely based on the actual gang rape and murder of two young Dalit women in 2014 in the rural hinterland of Badaun.

Chaitanya Tamhane's *Court* is about an elderly 'lower-caste' Dalit folk singer, Narayan Kamble, who is accused of sedition for his revolutionary song lyrics and hauled into a bureaucratic court battle. The boundaries between representation and reality are obliterated considering the film's lead actor, the late Vira Sathidar – a left-wing Dalit activist – was himself victimised and oppressed by the local police for several years. In the sequence leading to his arrest, Kamble utilises a public performance to lambast the government's neoliberal agenda decrying the 'religious jungles, racist jungles' and 'fancy malls' that typify the state's dichotomised master narrative – neoliberalisation and Hindutva nationalism (Devasundaram, 2018b, p. 161). Arguably, Kamble's radical song lyrics capture the structural reasons for the subaltern condition of the slum children in Tamil film *Kaaka Muttai/The Crow's Egg* – marginalised denizens in a national political project that has deepened the schism between rich and poor. Anusha Rizvi's *Peepli Live* is similarly cast against the backdrop of exploitative global multinational conglomerates such as American agrochemical and biotechnology behemoth – Monsanto, whose indiscriminate corporate operations in the Indian farming sector have been cited as a contributing factor to India's farmer 'suicide economy' (Shiva, 2013).

The suppression of dissenting political voices in the arts, as imagined in *Court*, is eminently visible outside the cinema sphere with the arrest of Tamil folk singer Kovan in 2018, for his song criticising Narendra Modi. His song lyrics invoke a wry reference to slippers in the Hindu religious epic the *Ramayana*, in order to critique the Tamil Nadu state government's subservience and sycophancy towards Modi's central BJP government: 'The story of a rule with slippers is in Ramayana. In Tamil Nadu Modi's two slippers rule' (Stalin, 2018).

Another instance of the BJP government's direct interference in cinematic expressions of political themes is the attempt to prevent YouTube from exhibiting the trailer for the crowdfunded documentary film *Lynch Nation* (2019) (Dutta, 2019). The film reveals the political underpinnings in the vilification of Dalits and mob lynching of several Muslim dairy farmers by Hindu cow protection vigilantes. This move by the Modi government illustrates how the independent documentary filmmaking sector is especially vulnerable to arbitrary state censorship measures, owing to some of these documentaries' more explicit non-fictional, social realist and activist approaches to topical political discourses.

Directed by Dalit filmmaker Neeraj Ghaywan, *Masaan* (2015) is a mosaic narrative film featuring multiple storylines set in the ancient Hindu pilgrimage town of Varanasi. The film reveals multi-layered social relations that intertwine with religion, caste, social divisions and politics. Akin to the Marathi films *Sairat* and *Fandry*, a story strand in *Masaan* features the inter-caste love affair between a pair of young star-crossed lovers. The strictures of caste that impede social equality and cohesion in modern India is echoed thematically in Ghaywan's direction of *Geeli Pucchi/Sloppy Kisses* which features an inter-caste liaison between a Brahmin and a Dalit woman. Overall, the geographical breadth covering representation of caste-related themes from Varanasi in the north, to Kerala in the south is reflective of the polyvocality of regional perspectives in the appraisal of socio-political problems via the Indies.

Caste dynamics are invoked in Indies such as the aforementioned *Peepli Live* and *Dekh Indian Circus* dealing with the themes of rural caste-based politics and the plight of impoverished Dalit farmer and tribal nomadic communities. *Chauranga* unravels the feudal landowner system and caste conflict in rural Bihar whilst *Serious Men* uses satirical comedy to chart the aspirational social mobility of a working-class Dalit man in metropolitan Mumbai. Thamizh's Tamil film *Seththumaan/Pig* (2021) unpacks the politics of meat consumption as a dividing line between caste groups – a theme directly relevant to the BJP's enforced ban on beef consumption in modern India.

Life of an Outcast bears distinctive aesthetic similarities to another independent Indian film – Gurvinder Singh's diegetically austere *Anhe Ghore Da Daan/Alms for a Blind Horse* (2011) which is a slow cinema meditation on the debilitated daily existence of an impoverished Dalit Sikh farming family in rural Punjab. *Life of an Outcast* is set in rural Uttar Pradesh, a northern Indian state currently under the authoritarian rule of militant Hindu monk turned BJP politician and state chief minister Ajay Mohan Bisht who refers to himself as Yogi Adityanath. The film's first aesthetic exposition is a political epigraph – 'This film is dedicated to all proletariats of the world and the people working against the Caste system'. In the film, a 'lower-caste' Dalit village schoolteacher is falsely accused by the 'higher-caste' school owner of teaching against the ideals of the Hindu holy epic, the *Ramayana*, and imprisoned in the local police station jail. This scenario, depicting arbitrary police arrest of Dalit individuals on spurious charges, is interpreted in other Indie films including *Court* and *Visaranai*.

Therefore, whilst Bollywood is an escapist and pleasure-based cinema of interruptions (Gopalan, 2002) that breaks rational and realistic narrative flow through mostly uncontextualised insertions of action set-pieces and sexualised song and dance interludes, the aforementioned disruptions in Indie films stand apart in their political function of issuing jolting and jarring reminders of the predicament of subaltern subjects.

Conclusion

The Indies have taken up the baton from their Parallel cinema progenitors as the distinctly political firebrands of contemporary Indian cinema. However, their largely unequivocal, uncompromising and confrontational approach to controversial and sensitive political themes sets them apart not only from Bollywood, but also from the more meditative, idealised and aestheticised realism of the earlier Parallel filmmakers. Emboldened by a globalisation sensibility that sees social media, cyberspace and the international film festival arena as sanctuaries from state censorship, the new Indies are outspoken in their challenging of the ruling order, religious orthodoxies and dominant social status quo. Whilst commercial Bollywood remains at the vanguard of the state's foreign policy of propagating Indian cultural soft power (see Chapter 4) and is therefore obliged to reproduce sanitised representations of India's contemporary zeitgeist, the Indies' location in an alternative space affords them more agency to articulate dissenting political narratives of resistance.

References

Anandan, S. (2016). CBFC declines to certify film. *The Hindu*. [online] Available at: www.thehindu.com/news/cities/Kochi/CBFC-declines-to-certify-film/article1 4510750.ece [Accessed 19 May 2020].

Chatterjee, S. and Rastogi, S. (2020). The changing politics of beauty labour in Indian cinema. *South Asian Popular Culture*, 18(3), pp. 271–282.

Devasundaram, A. (2018a). The subaltern screams: Migrant workers and the police station as spatio-carceral state of exception in the Tamil film *visaranai*. In: A. Devasundaram, ed., *Indian cinema beyond Bollywood: The new independent Indian cinema revolution*. New York: Routledge, pp. 257–280.

Devasundaram, A. (2018b). Beyond brand Bollywood: Alternative articulations of geopolitical discourse in new Indian films. In: R. Saunders and V. Strukov, eds., *Popular geopolitics: Plotting an evolving interdiscipline*. Oxon: Routledge, pp. 152–173.

Devasundaram, A. (2020a). Interrogating patriarchy: Transgressive discourses of "F-Rated" independent Hindi films. *BioScope: South Asian Screen Studies*, 11(1), pp. 27–43.

Devasundaram, A. and Barn, R. (2020b). Performativity of rape culture through fact and fiction: An exploration of India's Daughter and anatomy of violence. *International Journal of Cultural Studies*, pp. 1–19.

Dutta, A. (2019). Modi govt can't ban lynching documentary, so it plans to ask YouTube to pull down trailer. *The Print*. [online] Available at: https://theprint.in/india/modi-govt-cant-ban-lynching-documentary-so-it-plans-to-ask-youtube-to-pull-down-trailer/275887/ [Accessed 1 Sep. 2021].

Ghosh, A. (2020). Almost 50 years later, first Hindi film on queer love makes waves – Times of India. *The Times of India*. [online] Available at: https://timesofindia.indiatimes.com/india/almost-50-years-later-first-hindi-film-on-queer-love-makes-waves/articleshow/75916816.cms [Accessed 14 May 2021].

Gopalan, L. (2002). *Cinema of interruptions: Action genres in contemporary Indian cinema*. London: BFI Publishing.

IWCC. (2021). *Fowzia Fathima*. [online] Available at: https://iwcc.in/member/fowzia-fathima/ [Accessed 27 Aug. 2021].

Jaffrelot, C. (2021). *Modi's India: Hindu nationalism and the rise of ethnic democracy*. Princeton: Princeton University Press.

Jha, M. and Holland, O. (2020). 'Laxmii' critics say Bollywood blockbuster offers a problematic transgender portrayal. *CNN*. [online] Available at: https://edition.cnn.com/style/article/laxmii-bollywood-film-transgender/index.html [Accessed 20 Jan. 2020].

JKCCS. (2020). Kashmir's Internet Siege – an ongoing assault on digital rights. *Jkccs.net*. [online] Available at: https://jkccs.net/report-kashmirs-internet-siege/.

Kaur, P. (2017). Gender, sexuality and (Be)longing: The representation of queer (LGBT) in Hindi cinema. *Amity Journal of Media & Communication Studies*, 7(1).

Menon, A. (2019). Hail the Hindu Male! How Bollywood is selling Hindutva as history. *The Quint*. [online] Available at: www.thequint.com/voices/opinion/tanhaji-panipat-ajay-devgn-saif-ali-khan-marathas-hindutva-muslims-hindus [Accessed 1 Sep. 2021].

Osuri, G. and Zia, A. (2020). Kashmir and Palestine: Archives of coloniality and solidarity. *Identities*, 27(3), pp. 249–266.

OutlookIndia.com. (2020). *Kashyap upset over not getting Akhilesh-era sops: BJP*. [online] www.outlookindia.com/. Available at: www.outlookindia.com/newsscroll/kashyap-upset-over-not-getting-akhileshera-sops-bjp/1706080 [Accessed 1 Sep. 2021].

Rawle, S. (2018). *Transnational cinema: An introduction*. London: Palgrave Macmillan.

Seth, M. (2018). I used to call the BJP MLA Bhaiyya until he raped me. *The Indian Express*. [online] Available at: https://indianexpress.com/article/india/i-used-to-call-the-bjp-mla-kuldeep-singh-sengar-bhaiyya-until-he-raped-me-says-17-yr-old-unnao-girl-5135431/ [Accessed 31 Aug. 2021].

Shiva, V. (2013). *Seed monopolies, GMOs and farmer suicides in India- A response to nature*. Available at: www.navdanya.org/blog/?p=744.

Stalin, S. (2018). Tamil singer Kovan arrested for song criticising PM Modi, Rath Yatra. *NDTV.com*. [online] Available at: www.ndtv.com/tamil-nadu-news/for-song-criticising-pm-modi-trichy-police-arrest-tamil-singer-kovan-1837366 [Accessed 1 Sep. 2021].

3   Confronting censorship
Indies and the Central Board of Film Certification (CBFC)

A brief overview

Censorship in Indian cinema harks back to the British colonial era. Imperial authorities adopted film as a propaganda tool and endeavoured to thwart indigenous cinematic articulations that could stimulate dissenting, radical or revolutionary anticolonial public discourse (Chowdhry, 2000, p. 11). This was a systematised policy in occupied colonial territories as demonstrated in the ethos of the Colonial Film Unit (CFU) in British dominions in Africa. The CFU deemed the local natives too 'backward' to interpret their own culture, society and history. In India, the imposition of British Board of Film Censors (BBFC) rules in 1916 forbade 'scenes holding up the King's uniform to contempt or ridicule . . . subjects dealing with India, in which British Officers are seen in an odious light . . . or bringing into disrepute British prestige in the Empire' through content that could promote disaffection or resistance to the government (Bbfc.co.uk, 2021).

This colonial suppression of autonomous interrogative expression and reception through the medium of the moving image has to a significant degree been sustained by the preservation of British colonial laws and regulations in postcolonial India. The Cinematograph Act of 1918 has undergone several purported amendments in post-independence India including an ostensibly revised version in 1952. In actuality, several anachronistic and prohibitive stipulations largely remain intact in form, structure and function, with these subsequent amendments consolidating state control of censorship in the contemporary Indian cinema regulation regime.

The Central Board of Film Certification (CBFC) is the statutory presiding authority in matters relating to regulation and clearance of film content in India. No film is eligible for public distribution or screening unless it receives certification by the CBFC. The CBFC moniker deems to portray the organisation's primary role as the certification of films. However, the popular term 'Censor Board' used overwhelmingly by the Indian public

DOI: 10.4324/9781003089001-4

and often self-referentially by the CBFC itself indicates the actual function of the organisation. This censorial role is reflective of the CBFC's original title – Central Board of Film Censors – that was operational till June 1983. The Indian central government's Ministry of Information and Broadcasting has custodianship of the CBFC's structure and operations, rendering the CBFC an instrument of state power. Regardless of the vicissitudes in cycles of political power and irrespective of the political party in charge, censorship in postcolonial India has been conjoined to the state.

The CBFC comprises a hierarchical structure of advisory panels – the Examining Committee (EC), Revising Committee (RC) and the erstwhile Film Certification Appellate Tribunal (FCAT) – which was abolished by the BJP government in 2021. All CBFC members including the organisation's Chairperson are appointed by the central government. With its headquarters in Mumbai, the CBFC has nine Regional offices, one each at Mumbai, Kolkata, Chennai, Bangalore, Thiruvananthapuram, Hyderabad, New Delhi, Cuttack and Guwahati (CBFCindia.gov.in, 2021).

The Examining Committee (EC) is composed of individuals nominated and appointed directly by the Ministry of Information and Broadcasting. This practice of internal political appointments has constituted a bureaucratic breeding ground for nepotism and cronyism, where politicians often install into this crucial decision-making panel their associates, sympathisers and sycophants who are often devoid of the background, skills and acumen to appraise films. The EC acts as a gatekeeper to the CBFC censorship domain – the first point of contact for filmmakers submitting their work for certification. A film is examined, cuts or modifications prescribed and certification granted or withheld as per the prerogative of the panel members. The Examining Committee therefore wields immense power as the apex of the CBFC's tripartite structure to which filmmakers submit films hoping they will emerge from the censorship tunnel unscathed.

The Revising Committee (RC) is composed of a separate set of appointed members, often drawn from the Indian arts and cultural spheres. Second in the CBFC system, the power of the RC is diluted by a remit to only review films that have already been certified or have had redactions and modifications decreed by the EC. This limitation of freedom and agency attenuates the potential for impartial or independent appraisal of certified films handed down to the RC.

Third in line is the Film Certificate Appellate Tribunal (FCAT) involving retired high court judges and senior film industry figures. Prior to its abolition by the BJP government in 2021, FCAT served as the last recourse for filmmakers to appeal assigned certification, denial of certification or cuts and amendments prescribed by the EC and RC.

The certification model utilised by the CBFC has been interrogated for its ambiguity, dearth of age-specificity and overall ineffectuality. This rudimentary scheme includes the following categories:

U – unrestricted public exhibition
U/A – parental guidance for children under 12
A – restricted to adult viewing
S – restricted to specialist audiences such as scientists, doctors and engineers

Someswar Bhowmik (2013, p. 303) locates the Indian film censorship constellation as a hierarchical and bureaucratic political power nexus of 'advisory panels, Regional Officers, the Chairperson, CBFC and ultimately the Ministry of Information and Broadcasting'. Despite the high profile role of the CBFC chairperson, the fact that they are appointed by the central government renders them 'mere pawns in the political game that the state machinery and political parties play with the CBFC' (ibid.). Evidently, the system of political appointments and state control of the CBFC structure and function signposts a distinct lack of neutrality let alone autonomy in the purported process of film content certification. In this context, putative censorship undertaken by the CBFC plays a pivotal role in deciding the destinies specifically of independent films with politically polemical or alternative subject matter.

Censorship in India must not be framed as an exclusively top-down exercise notwithstanding the executive power wielded by the state through the CBFC as its censorship appendage. A de facto system of citizen-enforced self-censorship through moral and cultural policing and mob vigilantism has become entrenched, especially amongst religious and socio-politically conservative sections of Indian civil society. It is not uncommon for religious and nationalist organisations, ethnic, linguistic and caste groups and individuals to engage in subjective, spontaneous and heterodox modes of citizen-led censorship that can manifest in vocalised and violent registers of dissatisfaction against film content deemed objectionable.

Benchmark case scenarios in Indian film censorship link to extremist Hindu vigilante mobs vandalising cinema halls screening Deepa Mehta's lesbian-themed film *Fire* (1996), CBFC cuts to Shekhar Kapur's *Bandit Queen* (1994) for sex and violence, and the furore that followed Mira Nair's *Kama Sutra* (1996) whose representation of sexuality was decried both by the CBFC and social groups as being counter to Indian cultural values (Mehta, 2011, p. 56). Ironically, the film's detractors seem to have been oblivious of the Indian origin of the film's eponymous ancient sex treatise.

A predilection towards curbing and self-policing of free cinematic expression in the digital age appears to be the contemporary national sensibility:

> An overwhelming majority of Indians were in favour of censorship of online streaming platform services. A YouGov poll reveals that ninety percent of Indians agree "some form of censorship is required on platforms such as Voot, Netflix and Hotstar" to mitigate what they perceive as unsuitable content.
>
> (Kapur, 2020)

Conservative attitudes to representations of sexuality seem incongruous considering the celebration of polysexuality inscribed in the annals of Hinduism and etched in the eroticism of the ancient temples of Khajuraho. Preservation and continuation of colonial Victorian attitudes to sex seem anachronistic but are an embedded and dominant dimension of modern Indian society and culture. B. D. Garga (2005) traces the historical antecedents of moralistic and puritanical attitudes towards sexual intimacy on screen to the late 1940s:

> kissing disappeared from the Indian screen not because of a fiat of the censor but because of pressures brought on by social and religious groups. Heroines now had to be virgins and virtuous. Sexual appeal had to come from another quarter. In walked the vamp and the dancing girl, stereotypes that have survived.
>
> (Garga, 2005)

It is noteworthy that the modern Bollywood prototype of the sexualised song and dance 'item number' which scholars have identified as debasing in its objectification of women has remained largely free from CBFC censorship or censure from state authorities, religious figureheads, social and political groups and self-appointed moral guardians.

Social surveillance, moral guardianship and cultural policing have been propagated by significant sections of the Indian demographic susceptible to ideological instigation from dominant political and religious leaders with vested interests. This atmosphere of intolerance has intensified under the proto-fascist Hindutva ideology espoused by the ruling BJP government and its family tree of associated far-right organisations. Vigilante mobs affiliated to fundamentalist Hindu political and paramilitary groups ranging from the ideological fountainhead of the Hindu *sangh* (family) of political parties – the RSS – to militant wings such as the Bajrang Dal have with the collusion of police violently often fatally assaulted young couples for engaging in inter-caste and interfaith romances and marriages or for observing Valentine's Day. This theme has been investigated in Indie films such as *Masaan, Sairat* and *Kalla Nottam/The False Eye*. The amplified volubility of vigilante extremism has a direct impact on independent film creation in contemporary India and is corelated to the rise of religious hypernationalism and the dismantling of India's secular democratic constitutional principles in the last decade.

At the receiving end of these institutionalised and informalised mechanisms of censorship, the independent Indian filmmaking community along with progressive sections of scholars, activists, journalists, cultural representatives and judiciary have called repeatedly for an overhaul of the role and function of the CBFC. In 2016, the Shyam Benegal Committee led by the eponymous veteran filmmaker was constituted to reform the CBFC. Benegal's recommendation was for the CBFC to reflect its acronymic title and restrict its operation to certification rather than enforce censorship:

> The Committee is of the view that it is not for the CBFC to act as a moral compass by deciding what constitutes glorification or promotion of an issue or otherwise. The scope of the CBFC should largely only be to decide who and what category of audiences can watch the depiction of a particular theme, story, scene etc. . . . The CBFC categorization should be a sort of Statutory Warning for audiences of what to expect if they were to watch a particular film. Once the CBFC has issued this statutory warning, film viewing is a consensual act and up to the viewers of that category.
>
> (Shyam Benegal Committee Report, 2016, p. 7)

The Committee's report echoed inferences of a previous committee led by Justice Mukul Mudgal in 2013 and instituted by the Congress-led UPA government. The report cited numerous instances and scenarios where appointed members of the examining and revising committees had fallen short of the required standards of artistic evaluation and fair judgement of submitted films and inadequacy in ability to estimate the receptive impact of films on audiences. Akin to its 2016 counterpart, the Justice Mudgal Committee report commented specifically on a misconstrual of job specification by the CBFC:

> they perceive their role to be that of a Censor Board to cut and chop scenes and in some cases being affiliated to some political, religious or social group, impose without restraint, such political, religious or personal opinions upon content permissible in a film . . . the Committee came across complaints where panel members had objected to

use of words such as "boyfriend" or "kiss" used in a scene or even the uncharitably humorous representation of a political figure etc.

(Indialawnews.org, 2015)

Several scholars (Jaikumar, 2006; Mehta, 2011; Bhowmik, 2013) have presented erudite and meticulous accounts of the history of Indian cinema censorship and nuanced appraisals of the structural and procedural circuitry of the CBFC. The next sections of this chapter will therefore focus specifically on the censorship context applicable to the new wave of independent cinema spanning 2010 to 2021.

Censorship since 2010: situating Indie cinema in a broader context

Since the rise to prominence of the new wave of independent Indian films, censorship has been a focal point in their evolutionary trajectory. One of the key attributes that differentiates the Indies from Bollywood is alternative content – the Indies traverse wide-ranging themes from gender-based issues, LGBTQ+ narratives and caste-discrimination whilst often exposing the nexus between political corruption, mendacious tabloid news media and religious fundamentalism. These controversial and taboo themes place the Indies squarely in the censoring crosshairs of the CBFC.

Spanning a decade, it is important to take cognisance of the shifting Indian socio-political landscape since Narendra Modi's ascendancy to power in 2014. The ruling BJP has paved a populist pathway towards a unitarian Hindu nationalist identity concomitant with its thrust towards economic neoliberalisation – 'a model of entrepreneurial Hindutva' (Deb, 2018) through enticement of indiscriminate multinational corporate investment, crony capitalism and deregulation of the agricultural sector. The state has effectively taken control of the arts and culture sectors through directorial oversight of key organisations and initiatives such as the National Film Development Corporation (NFDC), International Film Festival of India (IFFI) and CBFC amongst others. This has been facilitated through strategic appointments of BJP affiliates and supporters at the helm of these organisations. This stratagem of state intervention in the creative and cultural infrastructure is mirrored by government manoeuvring in the educational sector, including India's publicly funded Jawaharlal Nehru University (JNU) and the Film and Television Institute of India (FTII), both renowned bastions of progressive left-liberal thought and expression. Therefore, it is essential to appraise censorship in contemporary Indian cinema as a coordinate in a complex matrix of political, social, economic, cultural, temporal, religious and ideological discourses. Specifically, cinema censorship in the age of new wave independent Indian films needs to be evaluated in the broader framework of a plethora of newly introduced laws and legislation designed to control and curb free speech, press and media freedom, civil liberties, citizenship and human rights.

Prominent among the aforementioned measures are the Citizenship Amendment Act (CAA) and the National Register of Citizens (NRC) legislated by the BJP government in 2019. The former was a thinly veiled attempt to exclude Muslim immigrants settled in India from claiming citizenship whilst the latter law proposed a nationwide census designed to expel 'illegal immigrants' by mandating individuals to furnish legacy records to ratify their Indian citizenship. The state's mobilisation to implement these enactments ignited vociferous protests across the nation.

Reflecting a marked deterioration in journalistic and media independence, India was ranked 142 among 180 in the Reporters Without Borders (RSF) 2021 World Press Freedom Index. Prime Minister Narendra Modi was included in a list of 37 heads of state or government identified as 'predators of press freedom' by the independent organisation (RSF.org, 2021). Underscoring the thesis that film censorship folds into a larger network, the BJP government has been implicated in an agenda to 'trample on press freedom by creating a censorship apparatus, jailing journalists arbitrarily or inciting violence against them' and has 'directly or indirectly pushed for journalists to be murdered' (RSF.org, 2021). State-abetted assassinations of outspoken journalists, activists and rationalists include Gauri Lankesh, M. M. Kalburgi, Narendra Dabholkar and Govind Pansare, to name a few among many (Deb, 2018).

Monumental changes to film censorship regulations at the behest of the ruling BJP government in 2021 also correspond to a time when draconian laws like the Unlawful Activities (Prevention) Act (UAPA) and National Security Act (NSA) are being invoked to suffocate even the simple act of organising protests or articulating opinions critical of the government which are deemed anti-national and punishable by archaic British colonial-era sedition laws.

Fr. Stan Swamy, an 84-year-old Jesuit priest and tribal rights activist, was arrested by the National Investigation Agency (NIA) on the basis of falsified documents planted on his computer. He became the oldest person to be charged with terrorism in India. Denied *habeas corpus*, medical care and basic human rights (Venkataramakrishnan, 2020), Swamy's death in 2021 from Covid-19 contracted whilst in prison was described as judicial and political murder. Fifteen other activists, poets, scholars, lawyers and human rights campaigners also arrested on fabricated charges of sedition in the Bhima Koregaon case continue to be imprisoned without trial. Similar scenarios of false imprisonment on charges of treason have been interpreted in

Indie films such as *Court* (2014) and Blue Sattai Maran's *Anti Indian* (2022) which was refused certification by the CBFC for its satirical assessment of religion and politics (Times of India.com, 2021).

Whilst appraising the specific cinema censorship scenario in contemporary India, it is imperative to take cognisance of the aforementioned rupturing transformations in India's socio-political and juridical fabric. The state's strategic conception and imposition of restraining legal precepts shackling freedom of the press and muzzling creative and artistic expression folds into the BJP government's larger master plan to rewrite India's secular democratic constitutional principles into a more authoritarian, theocratic and demagogic national narrative. In this sense, the BJP government's religio-political agenda and India's shift towards religious nationalism are directly relevant to the alternative and interrogative approaches of new independent Indian cinema.

Double standard: Bollywood and Indies

Bollywood films have been celebrated as mishmash 'masala' films – a cocktail of action, romance, melodrama and myriad other ingredients of affect-inducing visual spectacle. The soft power, cultural influence and political partisanship of the Bollywood industry to a dominant degree accords mainstream commercial Hindi films preferential treatment in the process of certification.

Big-budget Bollywood blockbusters routinely pass unscarred through the portals of the CBFC censorship labyrinth whilst politically incisive Indie films bear the disproportionate brunt of scrutiny, excision and proscription. Speaking during the release of *Anarkali of Aarah*, actor Swara Bhaskar criticised the CBFC for 'making things difficult for independent filmmakers who are trying to deal with brave topics' with the Censor Board vitiating Indie projects even prior to these films' release (Deccan Chronicle, 2017).

Whilst sex and violence have been the locus around which censorship in India has been oriented, Bollywood films featuring prurient 'item numbers' that debase and fetishise women and action extravaganzas celebrating gratuitous violence are regularly endorsed by the CBFC as family-friendly viewing. This could be linked discursively to the cult status gained by sexualised item songs which are celebrated as a form of Indian culture not only by domiciled Indians but also the non-resident Indians diaspora in western countries who cleave to item songs and ideologically patriotic Bollywood films as conduits to cultural identification and long-distance nationalism.

This is not to suggest absolutely all Bollywood films ipso facto circumvent the dogmatic censorship and certification process. On occasions when

Bollywood films take a cue from their Indie counterparts and attempt to push boundaries or challenge the ruling order and social status quo, they can become embroiled either in censorship quandaries or mob vigilante action. For instance, sci-fi satire critiquing religious superstition, blind faith, rituals and self-professed religious figureheads in the case of *PK* (2014) and female sexuality in *Veere Di Wedding* (2018) received opprobrium from conservative groups. A #boycottPK call was issued after the film was accused of 'maligning Hinduism'. Hindu fundamentalist groups Vishwa Hindu Parishad and Bajrang Dal sought a ban on the film and a First Investigation Report (FIR) was lodged against the director, lead actor and producer by the Secretary of the Hindu Legal Cell.

The on-location set of Sanjay Leela Bhansali's big-budget Bollywood film *Padmavati* was vandalised and the director attacked by a Hindu extremist group of the Rajput caste. The miscreants were acting on rumours that the film represented a romance between a historical Muslim king and the film's titular Rajput Hindu queen. Alongside vandalism of cinema halls and a moratorium on screenings in BJP-governed states, a regional BJP leader announced a cash bounty for anyone who would behead Bhansali and the film's female lead star Deepika Padukone (BBC, 2018). The CBFC ordered the film's title to be altered to *Padmaavat*. Ultimately, the Supreme Court reversed the ban on the film in BJP-ruled states.

In the decade since the Indies' evolution, Bollywood blockbusters espousing triumphalist ultra-nationalistic themes, valorising war against India's arch-rival Pakistan and promoting Hindu religious values and ritualistic practices as synonyms of Indian identity have been commercially successful and gained political patronage. *Uri: The Surgical Strike*, *Mission Mangal* and *PM Narendra Modi* released in 2019 and *Bhuj: The Pride of India* (2021) are examples of mainstream films that exploit the zeitgeist of populist nationalism pervasive in India. A clear example of Bollywood being co-opted into the BJP's populist playbook is Narendra Modi's public use of a slogan – 'how's the josh' (josh meaning passion or zeal) from jingoistic war drama *Uri: The Surgical Strike*. The catchphrase was brandished subsequently by BJP politicians and their followers known as *bhakts* (believers). Bollywood family sagas celebrating traditional Hindu *sanskari* values ranging from Karan Johar's *Kabhi Khushi Kabhie Gham* (2001) to Sooraj Barjatya's *Prem Ratan Dhan Payo* (2015) conform to the political ideology and vision of a Hindu nation propagated by the BJP government in 21st century India. Essentially, Bollywood films that appease the dominant political and national ideology largely bypass the censoring regime which reserves its authority for independent films whose content challenges the socio-political metanarrative.

Abolishment of FCAT: state-sanctioned structural paradigm shift

In a significant move in April 2021, the Film Certification Appellate Tribunal (FCAT) was annulled by the ruling BJP government. More liberal than the CBFC advisory panels, the FCAT has played an instrumental role in facilitating compromises with filmmakers and sometimes overruling CBFC decisions. For example, after significant national and international controversy, Alankrita Shrivastava petitioned FCAT and succeeded in gaining a release for *Lipstick Under My Burkha* albeit with several cuts to the film.

In another example of FCAT playing a crucial role in reversing decisions and remediating questionable practices by the CBFC, the Tribunal cleared the release of Kushan Nandy's *Babumoshai Bandookbaaz* (2017) after 'eight minor, voluntary cuts'. Incumbent CBFC chairperson Pahlaj Nihalani had ordered 48 cuts to the film after giving it an 'A' certificate, objecting to expletives in the screenplay and certain scenes (Firstpost, 2021). Other films cleared by FCAT include *Shaheb, Bibi, Golaam* (2016) and *Haraamkhor* (2017).

FCAT therefore provided a platform to independent filmmakers unsupported by the financial and influential power of big production houses to appeal against indiscriminate cuts and certifications without having to go through the circuitous route of litigation. As FCAT was composed largely of industry experts, filmmakers considered the Tribunal a preferable dispute resolution portal compared to judges in the Indian legal system. (Hirwani, 2021). In effect, the dissolution of FCAT could be interpreted as another decisively strategic move in the Modi government's masterplan to gain control of cultural discourse and stifle dissenting voices in the creative industries. The government's executive order deleting FCAT as a functioning film-specific court of appeal is denotative of the general curtailment of the freedom of speech and expression orchestrated by the BJP.

Following the abolition of FCAT, filmmakers have been directed by the government to register their appeals against CBFC certification at the high court, which can be a labyrinthine, protracted, expensive and bureaucratic process compared to the turnaround time previously employed by FCAT. According to an independent producer commenting anonymously:

> Producers aren't going to back stories that seem even vaguely risky because apart from being expensive, going to courts would also mean delays in release and no one wants that. More than the bigger producers, this would hurt the indie filmmakers. They anyway have such a tough time getting their films made, and now certifications will also become

an issue. These are the voices who tell different stories that reflect their views on society and politics, and that's what we'd be losing.

(Upadhyay, 2021)

Super censor laws: government (re)regulations, draft Cinematograph Amendment Bill 2021 and web streaming platforms

Subsequent to disbanding the FCAT, at the time of writing this book, the BJP government released a draft Cinematograph Amendment Bill on 18 June 2021, constituting another monumental paradigm shift in the regulation of Indian cinema. The proposed bill reconfigures the earlier Cinematograph Act of 1952 by according the Indian central government overweening powers to order revocation or re-examination of films already certified for exhibition by the CBFC and released in the public domain.

An editorial article in *The Indian Express* (2021) encapsulates Indian filmmakers' trepidation about the Cinematograph Amendment Bill 2021 which they perceive as an expropriative measure by the state to assume absolute power in the role of 'super censor':

> It empowers the Centre to revoke a certificate granted to a film by the CBFC, if it is found to violate Section 5 B (1) of the Cinematograph Act, 1952, which discourages certifying a film that is 'against the interests of [the sovereignty and integrity of India] the security of the state, friendly relations with foreign States, public order, decency or morality, or involves defamation or contempt of court or is likely to incite the commission of any offence'.
>
> (*The Indian Express*, 2021)

Specifically, the proposed amendment enables the Union government to order the CBFC chairperson to re-examine a certified film if the Union government receives a complaint or reference as to a violation of the aforementioned Section 5(B)(1) (Tankha, 2021). This proviso seems counter-intuitive considering it entails the state directing the CBFC to re-examine certification granted by the state-controlled CBFC in the first place. Importantly, the caveat of 'complaints or reference' prompting state reappraisal of a film and revocation of certification presents a façade of social consensus and public participation in this new form of super censorship. In reality, this facet of the amendment speaks to state foreknowledge of a readily available moral policing vigilante – political acolytes who are on call to supply complaints at the bidding of political powerholders. In other words, the amendment's appearance of being dependent on public consent is another democratic mirage for yet another draconian directive.

As reiterated in this book, the politically interrogative property of Indies is a hallmark that distinguishes them from mainstream Bollywood and renders Indie films more susceptible to the diktats of state-controlled censorship. The new, irrevocably political executive powers codified in the draft Cinematograph Amendment Bill 2021 pose a field of complexities in the future trajectory of the Indie filmmaking sector. The political content in Indie films therefore is likely to become even more entangled in the discursive coils of state intervention and amplifying erosion of India's secular constitutional credentials.

Under the revised regulation proposed in the Amendment Bill 2021, the formerly generic U/A category has been dissected into age-based categories: U/A 7+, U/A 13+ and U/A 16+. Significantly, this age-specific subdivision of the U/A category is applicable not only to films releases but is also a statutory classification for OTT (over-the-top) web streaming platforms. Mandating age-based certification to digital streaming giants such as Netflix and Amazon Prime Video is a conspicuous development in the arena of regulation and censorship in India where online platforms thus far were largely exempt from state censorship norms.

The revamped Cinematograph Amendment Bill 2021 also proposes to address piracy through imposition of an additional prison term for unauthorised recording of films in cinema halls. Reacting to this proposal, the Indian filmmaking community has sought more nuanced and holistic measures to address piracy rather than uniform punitive enforcement that neither accounts for varying circumstances and fair use nor provides substantive measures to deter illegal capture and proliferation of films at a systemic level.

Censorship in the digital domain

Narendra Modi's government has also initiated active steps to regulate and censor digital news media and video streaming platform content through promulgation of Information Technology (Intermediary Guidelines and Digital Media Ethics Code) Rules 2021. This new expanded ambit of IT Rules entailing state censorship of digital and social media content poses an adverse scenario for independent filmmakers. Emerging Indie filmmaker Samya Khanna states:

> The reason that most independent filmmakers prefer to go online is because the OTT (streaming) platforms act as a safety net. They can be

assured that the government won't play foul and take their art down. If the government steps in now, these creators or artists might be under constant threat if they are being vocal about unpleasant truths.

(Hirwani, 2021)

These transformational currents in the topography of Indian cinema censorship are a defining and rupturing moment. The widening of state censorship powers to include streaming platforms, digital social and news media in large measure synchronises with the apogee of authoritarianism under the Hindu nationalist BJP government since its ascendancy in 2014.

Netflix and Amazon Prime Video in addition to a range of national and regional streaming platforms significantly have filled the vacuum of an absent independent Indian Indie exhibition and distribution infrastructure. Until 2021, controversial films such as *Gandu*, *Unfreedom* and *Udta Punjab* have proliferated unpoliced on these online portals. The extension of censorship regulations to the digital domain raises important questions relating to continued autonomy of creative expression and the future of web platforms as a forum to present thematically divergent or controversial film content.

Specific case scenarios

Some contextual scenarios surrounding new independent films since 2010 may assist in interpreting the authoritarian model of state-imposed cinema censorship that has become normalised in 2021.

The anarchistic rap musical *Gandu* directed by Q is a quintessential early example of a new wave Indian Indie film mounting an iconoclastic challenge to traditional morals, cultural values and dominant social attitudes, particularly to sexual freedom. The film's graphic and defiant portrayal of unsimulated sex, full frontal nudity and profanity-laden screenplay rendered it an unprecedented benchmark in the annals of Indian cinema. The film's explicit content was therefore a priori antithetical to the CBFC rulebook, resulting in the film not gaining a certificate of release. Brandishing the 'banned in India' catchphrase as a selling point, Q utilised alternative avenues such as the international film festival circuit and a distribution deal with overseas companies to proliferate his film. In 2010, a bootleg version of the film was leaked on YouTube gaining 1.5 million viewers. This informal and unofficial mass access via the internet emphasised the inefficacy of the CBFC's hard-line policies of film regulation through censorship.

Similarly, Bengali independent film *Chatrak* (2011), directed by Sri Lankan filmmaker and Film and Television Institute of India (FTII) graduate

Vimukthi Jayasundara, was denied a theatrical release due to its sexual content as was the Malayalam film *The Painted House* (2015) whose portrayal of nudity was cited as the CBFC's reason for denying clearance. Raj Amit Kumar faced a similar situation with *Unfreedom*, which represented the taboo twin themes of a lesbian romance and religious extremism. When the film was denied a certificate of release by the CBFC, Kumar petitioned FCAT and ultimately appealed to the High Court which upheld the CBFC ruling. Akin to Q's alternative strategies of proliferation, Raj Amit Kumar disseminated *Unfreedom* through the global film festival network similarly deploying the 'banned in India' tag to promote the film. Eventually, *Unfreedom* was absorbed into the Netflix catalogue thereby circumventing the CBFC stipulations specific to theatrical exhibition.

Whilst *Fire* has become synonymous with censorship discourse surrounding its portrayal of a lesbian relationship between two Hindu sisters-in-law trapped in loveless marriages, the feminist orientation of *Lipstick Under My Burkha* entangled the film in a pitched battle with the CBFC. Alankrita Shrivastava's film, charting stories of four intergenerational women battling misogyny and socio-religious orthodoxy to gain freedom of sexual expression, was denied certification by the CBFC. Chairperson at the time, Bollywood producer Pahlaj Nihalani, a vocal BJP and Narendra Modi supporter, demarcated the film as being too 'lady-oriented'. Shrivastava was able to showcase her film across the international film festival circuit gaining media visibility, box-office success and critical acclaim for challenging a patriarchal and reactionary state-controlled Indian censorship machine. Shrivastava eventually took her case to FCAT which ordered the CBFC to grant the film an 'A' certificate after suggesting a few edits, facilitating an eventual Indian release of the film (Firstpost, 2021). Considered a watershed scenario in the censorship of Indian Indie films, *Lipstick Under My Burkha* is a bellwether film, exemplifying the CBFC's curtailment of female voices and the organisation's tacit upholding of the patriarchal and gendered national narrative synonymous with mainstream Bollywood films. Shrivastava has directed subsequent female-centric films including *Dolly Kitty and Those Twinkling Stars* (2019) and the Netflix series *Bombay Begums* (2021).

As mentioned, the CBFC has been particularly stringent and punitive on smaller low-budget independent films. Indie films confronting the politically controversial Kashmir issue have been particularly susceptible to CBFC censorship. Notable examples include *Harud* and *No Fathers in Kashmir*. Sanal Kumar Sasidharan's Malayalam film *Sexy Durga* was barred from screening at the International Film Festival of India (IFFI) 2017 by the Ministry of Information and Broadcasting. The film documents the road journey of a runaway interfaith couple – the titular young Hindu woman and her Muslim boyfriend and their encounter with entrenched social misogyny and bigotry. Declaring that the title of the film could 'affect law and order' and hurt 'religious sentiments' because Durga is the name of a Hindu Goddess, the Ministry of Information and Broadcasting and CBFC ordered the filmmaker to change the film's title to 'S Durga' (Saha, 2017). Marathi film *Nude* faced a similar predicament as *Sexy Durga* when it was expunged from the Panorama section of the International Film Festival of India (IFFI) for its portrayal of nudity.

Angry Indian Goddesses, marketed as India's first all-female road film, was beset by several cuts prescribed by the CBFC. These included screenplay references to the Hindu goddess Durga/Kali, sarkar (government), Adivasi (tribal), dildo and orgasm. Citing the anomalous scenario of the CBFC ordering excisions after the film was certified A – Adults only, the film's producer Gaurav Dhingra asserts:

> I don't know if there is censorship or certification, it's super confusing. . . . If there is censorship, then you should censor it at the script level, when not much money has been invested in the film. Why are you asking me for cuts after I have made the film? I have sold my house to make this film, why would I have made it in the first place if it had to be cut?
>
> (Mathew, 2015)

Although some of these Indie films eventually gain clearance, it is more often than not due to beleaguered and browbeaten filmmakers resigned to accepting prescribed cuts or making other allowances and compromises in the bigger picture of being able to release their work.

Another example, *Udta Punjab* investigates chronic drug abuse amongst young people in Punjab. Recalling some of the unflinching and transgressive aesthetic sensibilities of *Gandu*, the film's central character is a rock star Tommy (Shahid Kapoor) whose flamboyant cocaine-fuelled lifestyle invariably leads to sobering encounters with law enforcement. The film became a petri dish for the CBFC which prescribed an unprecedented 96 cuts to be made to the film when it was submitted for certification. Blurring lines between media, politics and cinema, the film became the epicentre of public sphere debate as a filmic exemplar of the degradation of 'Indian values and morals' through portrayal of debauchery and depravity.

Independent film directors, actors and producers have been at the vanguard of decrying the central government's totalitarian mobilisations in the form of annulling FCAT and initiating state revocation powers in the draft Cinematograph Amendment Bill 2021. Several film personalities expressed their disappointment at the FCAT abolition, including Vishal Bharadwaj, Guneet Monga, Devashish Makhija, Richa Chadha and Hansal Mehta who termed the state action 'arbitrary and restrictive' (Hirwani, 2021). Expressing anxiety and apprehension about what he perceives as a draconian design eminent Malayalam film auteur Adoor Gopalakrishan asserts:

> Now, the government plans to re-censor the censored films. This is against all norms of democratic functioning of institutions. When a regime suspects its subjects beyond reasonable limits, it smacks of authoritarianism. Intimidation and the feeling of being smothered are not what we expect from an elected government.
>
> (Venkiteswaran, 2021)

An open letter from 3000 notable members of the Indian filmmaking sphere expressing dissatisfaction with the revisionary powers proposed by the bill and requesting reinstatement of FCAT was dispatched to the Ministry of Information and Broadcasting (The Economic Times, 2021).

Conclusion

Censorship has been a close yet unsolicited companion to the new wave of independent Indian cinema. Filmmakers espousing alternative content do so with precognition that the systemic imperative of state-controlled censorship could result in dismemberment of their creative work. To a significant extent, the digital domain of YouTube, Vimeo and web streaming platforms presented a pathway to uncensored proliferation and access to unredacted film content. The BJP government's totalising restructuring of regulatory protocol extending the orbit of censorship to encompass the internet and streaming platforms in 2020–21 is a significant terrain-altering development. The overarching puissance of the Indian central government, particularly a religious fundamentalist BJP government whose goal is a Hindu theocratic state, augurs an even more restrictive field for divergent and non-mainstream film content.

Several Indian filmmakers have raised a collective voice against measures such as the elimination of FCAT and the super censor laws set in motion through the proposed Cinematograph Amendment Bill 2021. However, the seemingly inexorable implementation of these revisionist and unilateral state regulations augurs a complex path ahead for the Indian Indie film sector.

References

BBC. (2018). *Padmaavat: Why a Bollywood epic has sparked fierce protests*. [online] Available at: www.bbc.co.uk/news/world-asia-india-42048512 [Accessed 24 July 2021].

Bbfc.co.uk. (2021). *The BBFC from 1912–1949*. [online] Available at: www.bbfc. co.uk/education/university-students/bbfc-history/1912-1949 [Accessed 24 Aug. 2021].

Bhowmik, S. (2013). Film censorship in India: Deconstructing an incongruity. In: K. Gokulsing and W. Dissanayake, eds., *Routledge handbook of Indian cinemas*. Oxon: Routledge, pp. 297–310.

CBFCindia.gov.in. (2021). *About Us*. [online] Available at: www.cbfcindia.gov.in/ main/about-us.html [Accessed 24 Aug. 2021].

Chowdhry, P. (2000). *Colonial India and the making of empire cinema*. Manchester: Manchester University Press.

Deb, S. (2018). The killing of Gauri Lankesh. *Columbia Journalism Review*. [online] Available at: www.cjr.org/special_report/gauri-lankesh-killing.php [Accessed 24 July 2021].

Deccan Chronicle. (2017). Swara Bhaskar slams CBFC, lauds filmmakers covering brave topics in films. *Deccan Chronicle*. [online] Available at: www.deccanchron icle.com/entertainment/bollywood/070317/swara-bhaskar-slams-cbfc-lauds-independent-filmmakers-covering-brave-topics-in-films.html [Accessed 23 July 2021].

The Economic Times. (2021). *Film fraternity writes a letter to government for amending cinematograph act*. [online] Available at: https://economictimes.india times.com/magazines/panache/film-fraternity-writes-an-appeal-letter-to-govern ment-for-amending-cinematograph-act/articleshow/84055497.cms [Accessed 25 Aug. 2021].

Firstpost. (2021). Film certification appellate tribunal abolished; Filmmakers to now directly approach high court-entertainment news. *Firstpost*. [online] Available at: www.firstpost.com/entertainment/film-certification-appellate-tribunal-abolished-filmmakers-to-now-directly-approach-high-court-9503181.html [Accessed 22 July 2021].

Garga, D, B. (2005). *The art of cinema*. New Delhi: Penguin Viking.

Hirwani, P. (2021). Bollywood up in arms as India's film certification appeals process is scrapped without warning. *The Independent*. [online] Available at: www. independent.co.uk/independentpremium/world/bollywood-film-certification-appellate-india-b1827813.html?r=62558 [Accessed 8 Apr. 2021].

Indialawnews.org. (2015). Film censorship in India: The urgent need for reform by Mukul Mudgal. *India Law News*. [online] Available at: https://indialawnews. org/2015/10/01/film-censorship-in-india-the-urgent-need-for-reform-by-mukul-mudgal/ [Accessed 25 Aug. 2021].

The Indian Express. (2021). *Super censor*. [online] Available at: https://indianex press.com/article/opinion/editorials/new-cinematograph-amendment-bill-cen tral-board-of-film-certification-censorship-7381811/ [Accessed 25 Aug. 2021].

Jaikumar, P. (2006). *Cinema at the end of empire*. Durham: Duke University Press.

Kapur, M. (2020). More Indian men than women favor censorship of content on video streaming platforms. *Quartz India*. [online] Available at: https://qz.com/india/1739203/indians-for-censorship-of-hotstar-netflix-amazon-prime-content/ [Accessed 27 July 2020].

Mathew, S. (2015). What the CBFC didn't want you to hear in "angry Indian goddesses." *TheQuint*. [online] Available at: www.thequint.com/entertainment/what-the-cbfc-didnt-want-you-to-hear-in-angry-indian-goddesses#read-more [Accessed 25 Aug. 2021].

Mehta, M. (2011). *Censorship and sexuality in Bombay cinema*. Austin: University of Texas Press.

RSF.org. (2021). *RSF's 2021 "Press freedom predators" gallery – old tyrants, two women and a European | Reporters without borders*. [online] Available at: https://rsf.org/en/news/rsfs-2021-press-freedom-predators-gallery-old-tyrants-two-women-and-european [Accessed 24 July 2021].

Saha, P. (2017). Information and broadcasting ministry lashes out at allegations of intolerance over IFFI controversy. *India Today*. [online] Available at: www.indiatoday.in/india/story/information-broadcasting-ministry-iffi-controversy-sujoy-gosh-resigns-1086443-2017-11–14 [Accessed 25 Aug. 2021].

Shyam Benegal Committee Report. (2016). [online] Available at: https://mib.gov.in/sites/default/files/Shyam_Benegal_committee_Report_compressed.pdf [Accessed 25 Aug. 2021].

Tankha, R. (2021). *Why proposed amendments to the cinematograph act have left filmmakers unhappy*. [online] Available at: https://thewire.in/government/why-proposed-amendments-to-the-cinematograph-act-have-left-filmmakers-unhappy [Accessed 25 Aug. 2021].

Times of India.com. (2021). *'Anti Indian': Censor Board refuses to certify Blue Sattai Maran's film – Times of India*. [online] Available at: https://timesofindia.indiatimes.com/entertainment/tamil/movies/news/anti-indian-censor-board-refuses-to-certify-blue-sattai-marans-film/articleshow/81949313.cms [Accessed 24 July 2021].

Upadhyay, K. (2021). FCAT abolition will make releasing films even more tedious. *Firstpost*. [online] Available at: www.firstpost.com/entertainment/fcat-abolition-will-make-releasing-films-even-more-tedious-filmmakers-react-to-scrapping-of-censorship-appeals-body-9507491.html [Accessed 25 Aug. 2021].

Venkataramakrishnan, R. (2020). How does denying an 83-year-old undertrial with Parkinson's a straw and warm clothes serve justice? *Scroll.in*. [online] Available at: https://scroll.in/article/979601/how-does-denying-an-83-year-old-undertrial-with-parkinsons-a-straw-and-warm-clothes-serve-justice [Accessed 25 Aug. 2021].

Venkiteswaran, C. (2021). *The state has withdrawn all support of serious cinema: Adoor Gopalakrishnan*. [online] Available at: www.thehindu.com/entertainment/movies/the-state-has-withdrawn-all-support-of-serious-cinema-adoor-gopalakrishnan/article35320367.ece [Accessed 25 Aug. 2021].

4 Theoretical and philosophical approaches to the Indies

Introduction

This chapter suggests several epistemological, philosophical and conceptual frameworks that could assist the analysis of Indian Indie films. This is by no means a comprehensive compilation, as the hybrid, postmodern and evolving nature of the multifaceted Indies render them open to a range of intersectional, interdisciplinary and blended interpretive and critical approaches. The sections here highlight the possibilities of reading the Indies through the lens of politics and international relations, gender, sexuality, class, caste, power, technology, economy, philosophy and a range of other angles of approach and lines of flight. Indeed, bearing in mind the growing thrust towards decolonisation of dominant epistemologies, histories and institutional structures and concomitant endeavours to include more Global South perspectives particularly in western universities, this chapter hopes to stimulate independent, original and contemporary formulations, propositions, theoretical and philosophical paradigms to shape the future scholarly study and practice of new independent Indian cinema.

Soft power

Coined by American political scientist Joseph Nye (1990), this concept relates to the strategic use of cultural 'soft power' to coax countries to adopt American cultural sensibilities and products as an attractive alternative to using the coercive 'hard power' of military might and economic dominance. Despite its foundation as an Amerocentric paradigm, soft power has become universalised as an index to measure a nation's global cultural influence. Cinema has been instrumentalised in this regard – Hollywood in relation to the USA, the James Bond and Harry Potter franchises linking to the UK, and in the case of India, Bollywood has been conferred the role of national cultural soft power ambassador. Bollywood is now synonymous globally

DOI: 10.4324/9781003089001-5

as a byword or blanket term for all things Indian (Thussu, 2013). How is this relevant to the new wave of Indian Indies? As mentioned in the next section on Bollywood's meta-hegemony, the Indian state has brandished Bollywood as a totem of national cultural power on the global stage.

India's adoption of soft power to assist the nation's aspirations as an international economic superpower folds into the country's accelerated push towards globalisation. Whilst Bollywood has been promoted by the state as an instrument of Indian cultural soft power alongside yoga and tourism, the Indies battle for visibility and space against the hegemonic mainstream commercial Hindi film industry (Devasundaram, 2016a, 2018). The Indies also represent the multiple manifestations of globalisation in India through their socio-politically conscious state of the nation stories unveiling anxieties, schisms, instabilities and fragmentation that problematise Bollywood's fulsome and fantastical portrayal of a homogenised national narrative. Therefore, there are ramifications to and intersections between Bollywood's role as soft power agent and the Indies often interrogative and critical portrayals of India's subscription to neoliberalisation.

An understanding of 'brand Bollywood' (Devasundaram, 2016a) as a lucrative national cultural product peddled as soft power is therefore relevant to understanding the counter-narratives of the Indies which often focus on the discriminatory, divisive and detrimental aspects of the Indian state's abandonment of its erstwhile socialist and secular principles of the Nehruvian era in favour of a peculiar pastiche of post-liberalisation corporate and consumer culture and Hindu supremacist nationalism. The Indies therefore orchestrate the important function of puncturing the idyllic soft power bubble blown by Bollywood that presents an uncritical and illusionary vision of contemporary India as an ideal arranged marriage of neoliberal consumerism, middle-class aspirationalism and a rigidly orthodox Hindu religious, moral and value system.

India's soft power operates through double dimensions (Devasundaram, 2016a, 2018). The soft power story exported to the outside world presents India as a forward-facing progressive democracy attuned to free market economy trends and multinational corporate investment. The internal dimension of Indian cultural soft power preserves a sacralised and antiquarian image of India as innately and foundationally Hindu, sanctifying patriarchal values and adherence to strict dogmatic religious, social, moral and cultural codes.

This dualism is displayed by Bollywood in its global soft power operations. In its rumbustious efforts to gain wider audiences abroad, especially amongst the patriotic Indian diaspora in the USA, UK, Canada and Australia, Bollywood's soft power is hinged on selling the idea of Incredible India, the land of tigers, yoga, spiritual mystics, exotic colours, song and dance. This self-orientalising property in the soft power narrative spun by Bollywood is cheek-by-jowl with portrayal of oligarchs, business tycoons, industrialists, young entrepreneurs living lavish sybaritic lifestyles whilst adhering unswervingly to hyperreligious Hindu traditional and moral *sanskari* beliefs and rituals.

Indie films such as *Island City* (2015) are good examples of the *punctum* in the *studium* (Barthes, 1981) of a snapshot of modern India. Interrupting and rupturing the conventional Bollywood stereotype – the cliched *studium* of perceived Indian culture – several Indies foreground the voices of India's subaltern others – a disruptive *punctum* that punctures the halcyon glow of affluent indulgence privileged by Bollywood film representations. In the second story instalment in *Island City*, the notion of *sanskari* family values is excoriated through a satirical exposure of the patriarchal power and religious dogma that is the underpinning basis of *sanskari* sensibilities. Similarly, *Papilio Buddha*, *Raahgir*, *Parched*, *Photograph* and *Sir* inter alia through the POV of marginalised subaltern characters reveal monumental polarities between rich and poor and the ultimately alienating impact of the new neoliberal vision of India. In effect, these films pose the question – who really benefits from India's soft power strategies?

Therefore, the idea of Bollywood's overarching soft power can be appraised through the concept of the Indies as destabilising cinematic agents that critique if not undermine the romanticised and idealised portrayals essayed and disseminated by Bollywood both inside and outside India. The political predilection of several independent Indian films (Devasundaram, 2017) therefore brings to bear on their positioning in an interstitial space between India's own negotiation of tradition and modernity, spiritualism and materialism. The Indies therefore occupy a vantage in-between intermediary position – in the words of Frantz Fanon (1963, p. 227) a 'zone of occult instability' where new ideas, resistance and change can be negotiated. This location enables the Indies to challenge the dominant national narrative and cultural status quo that Bollywood due to its position as national soft power emissary is obliged to uphold.

Meta-hegemony

This is a bespoke theoretical model conceived originally in *India's New Independent Cinema: Rise of the Hybrid* (Devasundaram, 2016b) to provide a contextualised location of the Indian Indies in relation to Bollywood. As the pre-eminent popular culture proponent in India, the Bollywood industry wields significant power. The meta-hegemony refers to dominant and powerful film forms and industries that are part of a global hegemonic hierarchy in terms of exhibition, distribution and cultural soft power.

In essence, on a global cinema level, Hollywood exerts its dominance through global reach, visibility, commercial and cultural capital. Bollywood is a competitor to Hollywood, reaching diverse domains and markets including Egypt, Nigeria, China, the Middle East and Latin America. However, 'Bollywood' – the controversial moniker itself – is an imitative malapropism of the American industry's nametag and Bollywood is also still secondary to dominant Hollywood in terms of global capital generation, brand visibility and cultural soft power. In turn, Bollywood exerts its own internal dominance over the multifarious alternative and independent film sectors within India. These sedimented and inter-related layers of global film industry hegemony ripple into concentric circles of hegemonies – a meta-hegemony. How is this applicable specifically to the new independent Indian Indies? As has been explained in the early chapters, the new wave of independent films is enmeshed in the Bollywood ecosystem in terms of often relying on, negotiating with, encountering and contesting the hegemonic Hindi commercial film industry's financial, political, infrastructural, cultural and symbolic power.

Bollywood's internal meta-hegemony over the multifarious cinemas of India including the new Indies is manifested across three levels.

1   Bollywood largely dominates avenues of production, distribution, exhibition and marketing. Whilst Bollywood faces stiff competition from regional language commercial film industries in South India, namely the Tamil, Telugu, Malayalam and Kannada sectors, the fact that these vernacular industries are referred to as reductive facsimiles of Bollywood (akin to the term 'Bollywood' being an appellative forgery of 'Hollywood') – Kollywood, Tollywood, Mollywood and Sandalwood – demonstrates the ideological, symbolic and commercial dominance of mainstream Hindi cinema. Bollywood generates almost half of all box-office revenue despite producing only a fraction of India's prolific total yearly film output – 1800 films in 2018 (The Express Tribune, 2020). Bollywood's profitability is channelled through a monopoly of film finance and distribution in the form of corporate production houses devoted to blockbuster productions and often affiliated with dynastic Bollywood clans and celebrities, from Yash Raj Films, Eros International and UTV Motion Pictures to Karan Johar's Dharma Productions and Shah Rukh Khan's Red Chillies Entertainment. Distribution at local, national and global levels consolidates Bollywood's branding as a wide-reaching monolithic Indian cultural form, pervasive across northern Indian, but increasingly entrenched as the pan-Indian 'national' cultural common denominator.

As mentioned in Chapter 5, Bollywood has also been the mainstay of programming and exhibition in multiplex cinemas across India, often leading to the side-lining if not bypassing of Indie films. With its formidable financial repositories, star power and distribution networks, Bollywood also commands an impressive marketing and publicity machinery that spans print and social media, television and billboard advertisements and the music industry. This ecosystem normalising Bollywood as cinematic purveyor of monocultural India contradicts and erases the intrinsic diversity that underpins the multiple cinemas of India, including the new Indies.

2   The second facet through which Bollywood reinforces its status as custodian of Indian cinema and culture is the scripting of a homogenous national narrative that as stated earlier collapses the actual heterogeneity of India into a singular essentialised ideology. Bollywood has largely positioned itself as universal 'family-based entertainment' often under the totalising banner of majoritarian 'Indian morals and values' and a monadic Hindu cultural identity. In practice, the Bollywood industry is concentrated in Mumbai and the films are almost exclusively in Hindi, which is the dominant language of northern India and hardly representative of the polyglot southern and North Eastern Indian states. Bollywood has often been viewed dispassionately in south India as an unsolicited attempt to impose Hindi on a largely non-Hindi-speaking south. The dominating tendencies of the commercial Hindi film industry have been challenged regularly on linguistic, cultural and political levels by south Indian commentators and groups. In its film representation, Bollywood privileges the majority Hindu religion as the default norm despite India's status as a secular constitutional republic. Other conventional strategies to normalise majoritarian sensibilities as shorthand for 'Indian' culture include gendered roles for women who are often reduced to playing supporting or subservient roles or sexualised vamp figures. Religious and sexual minorities and so-called lower-caste Dalits are often caricaturised or overlooked in Bollywood films which fetishise a northern Indian ideal of fair skin and chiselled physiques as the onscreen archetype of pulchritude and beauty.

3   As discussed in the section on soft power, Bollywood has been sanctioned and endorsed by the Indian state as an instrument of Indian cultural soft power on the global stage. Bollywood film stars act as de facto political emissaries, spokespersons and representatives at several high profile international economic, cultural and political events. In general, to further its economic imperatives, the commercial film industry has tended to align with the executive policies, directives and decisions of any prevailing government. Narendra Modi and his BJP regime have

had vociferous support from a plethora of Bollywood producers, actors and other personnel. Prominent examples of avouched BJP votaries include Bollywood producer/director and erstwhile CBFC Chairperson Pahlaj Nihalani and actors Akshay Kumar, Vivek Oberoi and Kangana Ranaut. Ranaut, a particularly strident social media supporter of the Modi government's controversial policies, became embroiled in a Twitter dispute with pop star Rihanna, with Ranaut defending the BJP's unilateral legislation to corporatise India's agriculture sector – a state ruling that precipitated mass mobilisations of farmers who congregated in protest in Delhi in January 2021. The legitimisation of Bollywood as India's predominant cultural soft power implement has a significant impact on the Indies. Alternative themes and issues espoused by the new Indies often contradict or cut against the grain of the orthodox, nationalistic and majoritarian ideological narrative presented by Bollywood films. The Indies are therefore engaged in an uneven playing field and despite gaining ground noticeably, in terms of popularity, visibility and accessibility across urban centres in India, the Indies occupy an antithetical position to India's soft power story of entrepreneurial success, *nouveau riche* middle-class affluence and jingoistic nationalism spun by Bollywood and the Indian state. Indies are therefore affected disproportionately by the pro-Bollywood practices of multiplexes, film funders, press and media portals, cultural institutions and organisations, and also in significant measure, the Indian body politic. Contemporary Indian governments' strategic co-opting of Bollywood is a paradigm shift from previous Indian state patronage and promotion of Parallel new wave cinema across the 1960s–'80s which effectively positioned the arthouse Parallel film form as the national cinema of India. Since the shift towards free market liberalisation and consumer culture in the 1990s, Bollywood has usurped the position of 'national' cinema.

Understanding the dynamics of Bollywood's meta-hegemony would therefore be useful in interpreting the role of the new Indies in interrogating the dominant Bollywood imagination of Indian identity, culture, politics and society through the three facets of meta-hegemony elucidated in this section. The Indies' increasing gravitation towards international co-production and proliferation through web streaming portals Netflix and Amazon Prime Video could also be framed against the global dimensions of Bollywood's meta-hegemony. This is particularly relevant in a situation where the Indies are often impelled to look outward for infrastructural and financial assistance to gain international exposure and visibility in a global terrain where to a large extent all forms of Indian cinema are perceived reductively and erroneously as 'Bollywood'.

Glocalisation, urban space and subaltern other

In a contemporary zeitgeist, the urgent stimulus to confront issues of racism, gender violence, environmental degradation and socio-economic inequality has spawned radical global mobilisations, particularly over the coronavirus pandemic in 2020–21. During the decade of the Indies' evolution, movements including #MeToo and #MeTooIndia, Rhodes Must Fall, Extinction Rebellion and Black Lives Matter have gained global attention. In an era of decolonising epistemologies and discourse in the global landscape, it is important to devise and develop fresh and original interdisciplinary perspectives on intersecting local and global levels whilst appraising the Indian Indies.

Elsewhere, I have posited how film is a penetrating optic to interpret the rise of police brutality and urban violence on minority communities in India through a comparative lens including other Global South countries – Brazil and South Africa – whilst identifying connecting synapses of similar atrocities in USA and UK (Devasundaram, 2021). This network-based transglobal rhizomatic approach underpins my demarcation of four cinema-specific conceptual reference points – interpellation, interpretation, intersectionality and imagination.

Interpellation is the insertion of the film spectator into a junction of their own perspective and the point of view of film characters to negotiate onscreen portrayals of political, gender-based and other forms of violence. Interpretation is the film's figurative (re)construction of urban violence – the ideological standpoint, formal and stylistic cinematic approaches to representing urban violence. Intersectionality relates to the ability of film to grapple simultaneously with multiple themes of race, ethnicity, identity, gender, caste, class and sexuality. Regarding imagination, films can present the possibility of imagining resistance, offering strategies to challenge state-orchestrated violence and demand reform. This film analysis framework is directly applicable to incisive Indian Indies which present interrogative and critical appraisals of the political state of play in India through a globally accessible film grammar.

Another mode to analyse the Indies is through their imaginations of a global-meets-local – *glocal* – network society. Several Indie films adopt the hyperlink multi-narrative film format often against the canvas of the big metropolises – Neil Narine's (2010) interpretation of the 'city film' is pertinent in this regard. Prominent cosmopolitan centres such as Mumbai, Delhi, Kolkata, Chennai and Bangalore have been explored in postmodern mosaic narrative films such as *Dhobi Ghat*, *Kathaah@8*, *I Am*, *Visaranai*, *B.A. Pass*, *The Lunchbox*, *Photograph*, *Bangalore Days*, *Lucia* and *Ajeeb Daastaans*. Regional, small town and rural local perspectives have often been incepted into film narratives such *Peepli Live, Raahgir/The Wayfarers, Article 15, Thithi, Life of an Outcast* and *Sherni*, often to demonstrate the presence of the rural other in the urban self. It is therefore possible to conflate Arjun Appadurai's (1996) thesis of multi-layered global cultural flows across ideoscapes, technoscapes, mediascapes, financescapes and ethnoscapes with the Indies' interpretations of globalisation and its impact in contemporary India.

Subaltern urbanism (Roy, 2011; Devasundaram, 2020a) is another pertinent template to ponder on themes of socio-economic inequities that punctuate Indian independent films' narrative navigation of glocalising currents as exemplified in films such as Geetu Mohandas's *Moothon/The Elder One*, Dipesh Jain's *In the Shadows*, Nabamita Ghosh's *Chegu*, M. Manikandan's *Kaaka Muttai/The Crow's Egg*, Devashish Makhija's *Ajji*, Ruchika Oberoi's *Island City* and Nicholas Kharkongor's *Axone*. *In the Shadows*, set in the labyrinthine alleyways of old Delhi, provides a vicarious sensorial experience of existence in confined local spaces as does *Axone*, about a group of young friends from the North Eastern state of Nagaland dealing with socio-cultural and ethnocentric prejudice as migrant workers in Delhi. Right to space and the city (Lefebvre, 1991; Harvey, 2012) are important analytical concepts identifiable in several Indies, particularly in terms of their representation of marginalised, oppressed and precarious individuals and communities. The iconic yet moribund Irani cafes associated with the minority Zoroastrian Parsi community and synonymous with the historical and cultural heritage of Mumbai are foregrounded in *Dhobi Ghat* as spaces under threat of extinction with the rise of commercial cafe franchises in India. It is possible to observe in several Indie film narratives the culturally specific modes through which dispossessed, destitute and disempowered subalterns summon alternative strategies, workarounds and hacks, utilising meagre immediately available resources and transforming them into inventive workable solutions – an informal practice referred to as *jugaad* (Rai, 2019) in indigenous parlance.

Gautam Bhan (2019) encourages 'expansion of a vocabulary of Southern urban practice' that speaks to an amplifying body of urban theory from the Global South that 'insists on calling out hegemonies of knowledge and dominant forms of practice no matter where they emerge' (Bhan, 2019, p. 642). Informal practices of living in Indian urban spaces are visualised in films such as *Serious Men, Ship of Theseus, Lucia* and *Photograph*. Taking into account the conceptual frameworks mentioned so far, the Indies could be evaluated through interconnected templates of urban space and subaltern identity. The concept of the city as heterotopia (Foucault, 1986; Devasundaram, 2020a) where dominant and marginal discourses and their representatives collide and coalesce is concomitant with questions regarding the right to the city – who has access to the city's spaces; who has a say in the production of the city's space; and who controls dominant urban narratives that act as significations – the grand narrative of the city?

Similarly, the Indies also blend locally specific aesthetics with social realism to espouse *local realism* (Devasundaram, forthcoming in 2022) as visualised in films such as *The Great Indian Kitchen* rooted in Kerala, *Life of an Outcast* in rural Bihar, *Evening Shadows* in Karnataka and *Hamid* set amidst the conflict in Kashmir. All the films cited in this section underscore the glocal ethos of the Indies and the potential to drawn on globalisation and urban socio-spatial theories as conceptual touchstones for filmic analysis.

F-Rated perspectives

Scholars note how 'Bollywood from its inception has been male dominated' locating the commercial film sector as 'a place where patriarchal and misogynistic culture prevails' (Mishra, 2021, pp. 57–58). The Indies are distinctly different from Bollywood in their portrayal of strong roles for women both behind and in front of the camera. In this context, feminist interpretive frameworks could be summoned to gain deeper understanding of onscreen representation of gender-based themes and female identity as well as industry codes of practice in relation to gender dynamics in the contemporary Indian filmmaking sector in general.

Western templates such as the Bechdel test devised by Alison Bechdel serve as a simple but useful barometer to evaluate levels of female representation in film. The benchmark of the test involves representation of two women in a film who speak to each other about any topic other than a man. In 2014, the F-Rating was conceived by festival director Holly Tarquini at the Bath International Film Festival. The F-Rating is accorded to a film whose director, screenwriter and lead actor are female. As asserted in the article *Interrogating Patriarchy: Transgressive Discourses of 'F-Rated' Independent Hindi Films* (Devasundaram, 2020b), several new Indian Indie films meet the requirement of a bona fide F-Rating. Examples include Anu Menon's *Waiting* which was created by a preponderantly female production team. *Toofan Mail* is scripted, directed and stars Akriti Singh. *Island City* is written and directed by Ruchika Oberoi and features prominent Indie actors including Tannishtha Chatterjee and Amruta Subhash; Alankrita Shrivastava's *Lipstick Under My Burkha* and Leena Yadav's *Parched* all exemplify the F-Rating criteria. In a significant detour from Bollywood, the independent new wave has also released a range of female-centric films directed by men including *Sherni* by Amit Masurkar, *Angry Indian Goddesses* by Pan

Nalin, *Soni* by Ivan Ayr, Aditya Kriplani's *Tikli and Lakshmi Bomb* and Jeo Baby's *The Great Indian Kitchen.*

Laura Mulvey's (1975) seminal essay *Visual Pleasure and Narrative Cinema* has served as a bellwether for interrogating the male gaze and the objectification of women onscreen. Although Mulvey's focus is on European and American paradigms, her thesis is particularly applicable to Bollywood's normalisation of the sexualised song and dance sequence – the 'item number'. However, feminist readings of new independent Indian films must be undertaken from an inclusive array of scholarly standpoints at the intersection of western and Indian feminist and postfeminist debates. This is particularly important considering 'women of colour's critique of the racist and ethnocentric assumptions of a largely white, middle-class feminism' (Brooks, 1997, p. 8). Defiant articulations of female sexuality in Indie films *Bulbul, Lipstick Under My Burkha, Anarkali of Aarah, Tikli and Laxmi Bomb, Parched* and *Unfreedom* present a strong case for the reclamation of sexual identity, empowerment and emancipation by marginalised and debased female figures stigmatised and denigrated by Indian society. Sex workers in *Tikli and Laxmi Bomb* are therefore accorded autonomy and agency and are humanised in the film. The intergenerational quartet of women *in Lipstick Under My Burkha* combat patriarchal order in their quest for sexual expression despite facing a violent backlash – the postfeminist quandary of transformative female liberation facing the brick wall of an intractably misogynistic social sphere. Uma Narayan's (1998) thesis of postcolonial feminism highlights the inadequacy of a culturally essentialist white western heterosexual middle-class feminist paradigm when wielded as a one-size-fits-all model to interpret women's diverse lived experiences in specific South Asian contexts. This is especially valid considering the multiple domestic and social roles undertaken by female characters portrayed in Indian Indie films. Examples include Konkona Sen Sharma's portrayal of Shirin – an all-in-one Muslim housewife, mother and clandestine career woman in *Lipstick Under My Burkha* – and Nandita Das's character Afia in *I Am* who confronts social stigmatisation by taking a post-divorce decision to become a single mother via IVF treatment.

In essence, female identity as portrayed in Indian Indie films is innately multifarious and nuanced. This resonates with the intersectional approach undertaken by Indie films which may focus on a specific theme or issue such as gender, caste, politics, sexuality or religious identity but nonetheless reveal a network of overlapping discourses that problematises any mono-dimensional or essentialised interpretation of female identity. For instance, Vidya Balan's character Vidya Vincent in the film *Sherni* is presented as a Christian Malayalee from Kerala in an interreligious marriage with her north Indian Hindu husband. Tillotama Shome in *Raahgir/The Wayfarers* is the female breadwinner of an impoverished Adivasi tribal family whose hand-to-mouth existence is the result of the family's subaltern status and exploitation by the rapacious mining corporation that has expropriated the Adivasi community's land. These local grassroots perspectives and layered narratives of female being, status and lived experience at both the marginal rural and cosmopolitan centre of India are represented in a gamut of Indie films and are open to specific and balanced appraisal from a blend of exogenous and endogenous scholarly perspectives.

Gayatri Spivak's seminal essay *Can the Subaltern Speak?* (1994) is subtended by the thesis that the doubly colonised (first by British colonial occupation followed by postcolonial socio-cultural patriarchy) South Asian female subaltern is rendered doubly silent. In this context, several women subaltern characters in Indie films not only speak up against but also perform acts of resistance against prevailing oppressive domestic and social conditions. The emergence of independent Indian feminist film organisations such as Ektara Collective and Women in Cinema Collective (WCC) which was formed in response to the 2018 #MeTooIndia movement necessitates inclusion of contextualised local perspectives in corresponding scholarly appraisals.

In summation, the Bechdel test and the F-Rating are valuable interpretive indices to evaluate new independent Indian films as well as guide film programming and curation practice generally. However, it is essential to engage simultaneously with several intersectional contemporary modes of analysis that account for the disjunctions, synergies and specific historical contexts between feminist and postfeminist epistemologies, from both indigenous Indian and western standpoints.

Queer studies

The independent film sector has been a pivotal platform for articulation of narratives engaging with taboo themes relating to the spectrum of LGBTQ+ identities in contemporary India. Queer theory concepts including the performativity of gender (Butler, 1990) and the categorisation and control of homosexuality as a discourse that amalgamates sexuality, knowledge and power (Foucault, 1978) are themes that can be applied to critical reading of a spectrum of independent films. *Fireflies* (2019) deals with the gender reassignment journey of a gender dysphoric young man who identifies as female but experiences daily vilification in her village in Assam where she is referred to pejoratively as 'lady'. Similarly, B.S. Lingadevaru's *Naanu Avanalla . . . Avalu/I am Not He . . . I am She* (2015) is a low-budget

Kannada film set in Bangalore and based on the life of transgender female actor and Dalit activist Living Smile Vidya. *Aligarh* (2016) unpacks the discursive entanglement of power and knowledge when a university professor is outed as gay by a news media channel. The navigation of private and public spaces, identity formation and individual freedom through media is pertinent in an arena of amplified collusion between right-wing tabloid Indian news channels and the ultranationalist machinations of political power in BJP-ruled India. Rohit Dasgupta (2017) locates a domain of digital queer identities being mediated through online platforms including social media, dating apps and websites reflective of the new terrain of LGBTQ+ identity formation in virtual spaces, especially in urban India.

Whilst Rajinder Dudrah (2012, pp. 45–46) consolidating Ashis Nandy's (1998) paradigm identifies as a 'secret politics' of gender and queer sexuality Bollywood's notoriously tongue-in-cheek, tangential and often disparaging references to same-sex desire, it is the new wave of independent Indian films that have shattered this smokescreen of secrecy and brought queerness out of the closet. The #ComeOutandQuestion catchphrase adopted as a promotional tag for *Aligarh* exemplifies the Indies' awareness of the discourse-generating potential of the digital sphere and the Indies' open advocacy of LGBTQ+ rights.

Karan Johar, a gay Bollywood producer/director who has consistently been cryptic about his sexuality, has been criticised for his early films' typecasting and lampooning of gay characters although his more recent productions *Bombay Talkies* and *Ajeeb Daastaans* have extended substantive and nuanced portrayals. Whilst homoerotic bromances have been represented in Bollywood films ranging from the iconic *Sholay* (1975) to *Dostana* (2008) about two straight men pretending to be gay, the release of the first mainstream commercial Bollywood films to deal openly with lesbian and gay identity – *Ek Ladki Ko Dekha Tho Aisa Laga* (2019) and *Shubh Mangal Zyaada Saavdhan* (2020) – attest to the shifting attitudes in Bollywood to LGBTQ+ representation. To a significant extent, credit is due to the influential Indie new wave which has been championing equal rights for sexual minorities through candid representations of same-sex desire and relationships.

With the decriminalisation of homosexuality in 2018, the pathway to accentuated representation of queer stories seems logical, particularly in the Indie sector. However, the tightening of state censorship regulations and rise of religious fundamentalism in India under the BJP is likely to counteract the newfound freedom of expression although this is precisely the restrictive conditions in which bold independent filmmaking can thrive. Cultural specificity whilst assessing LGBTQ+ identity and discourse in India is a sine qua non as exemplified in *Aligarh* when lead character Prof.

Siras is bemused when he is categorised by the media as 'gay' – finding the three letters an inadequate signifier to define the ocean of poetic emotion and experience of love.

In this sense, the categorisation schema and classificatory lexicon normalised in the west is still alien especially in rural regions and smaller towns in India. The act of coming out universalised in the western world is fraught with complexities and danger in an Indian context, where the ideological 'tyranny' of the (heterosexual) family apparatus (Althusser, 1972) reigns supreme and the inescapable norm of marriage is idealised. The theme of homosexual identity in rural and small town India is perennially underexplored in feature-length fiction films. Independent features such as Sridhar Rangayan's *Evening Shadows* focusing on a young man coming out to his ultra-orthodox Brahmin parents, *Kattumaram/Catamaran* charting a lesbian romance in a remote fishing village in deep south Tamil Nadu and the aforementioned *Fireflies* set in Assam delve into hidden homosexual and transgender lives in untrodden rural and semi-urban zones. These films could therefore be evaluated as examples of local realism that can help in contextualising and unpacking complex and multi-layered cultural, social and religious factors that must be factored in any reading of LGBTQ+ narratives specific to an Indian scenario.

There is rich scholarly scope to formulate deeper understanding of local perceptions and classifications of the gender spectrum and sexual identity in the Indian context and the intermeshing discourses that blur borders between local, national and global.

Post-cinema and production culture

Production culture and distribution systems constitute an understudied and underestimated dimension of Indian film studies. A production and digital distribution approach to analysing the evolution of new Indian Indies could be adopted from a post-cinema standpoint. It is particularly true in the case of new independent Indian films that 'digital networks make the marginalized film easily available' (Hagener, Hediger, and Strohmaier, 2016, p. 7). A glance through the Netflix catalogue reveals an impressive assortment of new wave independent films spanning 2010 to the present. Increasing dominance of the digital domain in the form of OTT (over-the-top) streaming services such as Netflix and Amazon Prime Video and fissiparous modes of audience reception through multiple technological devices and formats render it essential to interpret the Indies through these emerging digital landscapes of production, distribution and exhibition.

Alongside the advent of new wave independent Indian cinema, a new digital constellation of film production and proliferation has also recalibrated the role of film producers, editors, cinematographers and other filmmaking professionals. Dynamic independent producers such as Guneet Monga, founder of Sikhya Entertainment, have been at the vanguard of influential Indie films such as *Gangs of Wasseypur*, *The Lunchbox* and *Masaan*. The shifting terrain necessitates working across multiple networks and versatile production and distribution conduits traversing OTT platforms to television, film festivals and theatre releases. The glocal disposition of independent Indian films has entailed transnational collaboration on creative as well as logistical production and distribution levels. It is not uncommon for postproduction or sound design for Indian Indie films to be conducted overseas. For instance, Indo-German production *Qissa* (2015) directed by Anup Singh had a simultaneous multiplatform release in cinemas, on DVD and video-on-demand, backed by an intensive online and social media marketing strategy. Indian-themed Netflix web series such as *Selection Day* (2018) adopt international production culture with executive producers based in Los Angeles, director and editors in London and film crew in Mumbai.

John Caldwell's (2008) research on critical industrial practice is a useful touchstone although its limitation to Hollywood necessitates a more localised and industry-specific study that accounts for variances and particularities in the contemporary Indian film production context. The idea of a post-media aesthetics could be conflated with the slick visual template and production values of Netflix – a 'Netflix aesthetic', which has become standardised in web series and Netflix-commissioned films.

Smith Mehta (2019, p. 5557) extends a probing study on 'nepotistic tendencies of traditional media' where bias towards individuals with mainstream industry connections, established reputation and revenue-generation track record can minimise opportunities for talented newcomers. In this scenario, filmmakers without prior association with or links in the film industry are availing of digital platforms and social media to showcase their content. Increased digital video consumption has also attracted interest from media businesses, as evidenced by around 40 Over-the-Top (OTT) platforms streaming in India. Reports predict that India is on course to be amongst the top 10 OTT markets globally by 2022 (PWC/ASSOCHAM, 2018, p. 39).

In a digital age of cross-platform content creation and consumption that blurs borders of film, television, web streaming and social media, the decentralisation of conventional cinema releases has had an impact on alternative content generated from the independent filmmaking sector. Indie feature films since 2010 have served as the template for the expanded format of web series such as *Sacred Games*, *Paatal Lok*, *Selection Day*, *Tandav*, *Family Man* and *Bombay Begums*, all of which feature recognisable creative and production personnel from the independent domain. With Indies increasingly populating the roster of Netflix and Amazon Prime Video and indigenous web series erasing boundaries between film and television, the transglobal practices of production culture is an emerging arena of focus. Mehta (2019, p. 5563) identifies the need for bespoke research on 'the labor practices among the television, film, and digital media to rightfully assess the medium-specific benefits that the creators derive from working in each of these mediums'. The increasing trend of direct-to-digital film releases has been spurred by the Covid-19 pandemic situation, and the decline of DVD releases begets the question of concentrated power in the hands of streaming platforms which could potentially constrict egalitarian access to films especially across the global education sector.

Multimodal access to films on OTT platforms, film festivals, mobile phones, laptops and conventional cinema screens opens multiple avenues to assess the dynamic landscape of digital, conventional and hybrid modes of production and distribution in the Indian independent film sector.

Dalit studies

One of the conspicuous characteristics that distinguishes the Indies from Bollywood is their representation of subaltern characters and communities. The Indies present a range of subaltern stories from the point of view of powerless, dispossessed, marginalised and oppressed people. Central amongst this assemblage of storylines featuring othered individuals and social groups is the issue of caste discrimination which is a singular socio-religious and political system specific to India.

Scholars such as Isabel Wilkerson in her book *Caste: The Origins of our Discontents* (2021) have endeavoured to conflate caste stratification and caste-based oppression with racial segregation in the USA. Whilst there are several pertinent inferences and significant applicability in Wilkerson's interpretation, the malaise of caste indubitably has its roots in the religious bulwark of Hinduism's obdurate labour division structure. In this sense, the complex performative and operative manifestations of caste discrimination are tethered specifically to an Indian context.

The so-called lower-caste Dalit community, formerly referred to as 'untouchables', according to religious dogma are placed at the bottom of a caste system that positions the 'priestly class' of Brahmins at the top. Dalit communities still countenance entrenched social, religious and political prejudice, oppression and debasement in contemporary India. Across their evolutionary timeline, new independent Indian films have exposed multiple dimensions of the Dalit struggle for equality.

Dalit film director Neeraj Ghaywan introduces as a strand in his mosaic narrative film *Masaan*, a cross-caste teenage relationship between a young Dalit man Deepak (Vicky Kaushal) and a 'high-caste' teenager Shaalu

(Shweta Tripathi). Deepak's caste designation dictates his daily occupation of burning corpses on funeral pyres in the ancient Hindu town of Varanasi. Ghaywan also directed *Geeli Pucchi/Sloppy Kisses*, one of the story segments in the anthology Netflix film *Ajeeb Daastaan*s. *Geeli Pucchi* centres on a Dalit lesbian blue-collar worker Bharti (Konkona Sen Sharma) in a male-dominated factory. Bharti enters into a romantic relationship with her new work colleague – an 'upper-caste' Brahmin woman Priya (Aditi Rao Hydari) who eventually gains the white-collar administrative job for which Dalit Bharti is bypassed, despite her proven skills and experience. *Serious Men* (2020) is another film example that foregrounds Dalit lived experience. The act of challenging dominant Bollywood's beauty archetype by casting 'darker-skinned' female and male actors such as Tannishtha Chatterjee, Nandita Das, Konkona Sen Sharma, Nawazuddin Siddiqui and Omkar Das Manikpuri as 'lower-caste', working-class or rural characters in leading independent film roles is a distinct riposte to Bollywood's colourism and fetishism of fair skin mirrored in endorsements of skin whitening creams by several Bollywood superstars including Shah Rukh Khan, Hrithik Roshan and Aishwarya Rai.

Dalit Studies as an emerging disciplinary area could be adopted to investigate Indie film representations of Dalit discourse. In his book *Caste Matters* (2019) and article on *Dalit Cinema* (2018) Dalit scholar Suraj Yengde identifies a 'Neo-Dalit rising':

> the Indian film industry is an inherently caste-based, biased, mechanised product of technological industrialisation in which Dalit inclusion is not a moral concern. The mainstream film industry in India delivers the desires and principles of market and society by excluding a Dalit framework outright – a problem now being addressed by the entry of an explicitly Dalit cinema.
>
> (Yengde, 2018, p. 503)

Yengde proceeds to illustrate his thesis of a new Dalit cinema through illustrative examples of two seminal Indie films in Marathi by Dalit writer/director Nagraj Manjule – *Fandry/Pig* (2013) and *Sairat/Wild* (2016). Both films received critical acclaim and box-office success and have acted as filmic bellwethers for the unequivocal Dalit cinema that has emerged from the independent film domain.

Often, the navigation of caste identity in Indie films is melded with other discursive strands relating to gender, sexuality and politics. For instance, in *Raahgir/The Wayfarers*, female lead character Nathuni (Tillotama Shome) from an Adivasi tribal ethnic background is a daily wage labourer and sole breadwinner for her family. In a flashback sequence, the narrative reveals how Nathuni's husband was rendered paralysed from the waist down by a bullet fired by security guards dispersing the local tribal community protesting against appropriation of their land by a mining corporation. The film's interlinking of tribal Adivasi lived experience with the broader framework of economic and political exploitation in neoliberal India points to the intersectional ethos of Indies whose engagement with caste invariably conjoins with multiple other forms of alterity. Similarly, *Papilio Buddha* presents a Dalit-driven perspective on the rapining of Dalit land by the government through its repressive law enforcement and unscrupulous political agents. The film features Dalit activists and social groups and critiques Indian political icons such as Mahatma Gandhi whilst engaging concurrently with themes of same-sex desire and caste-based sexual violence inflicted on Dalit women.

Eminent Dalit scholar and human rights campaigner Anand Teltumbde asserts in *Dalits: Past, Present and Future* (2017, p. 160) that 'Hindutva is a political movement of the Brahmanical upper castes in India that seeks to revive the ancient Hindu order'. This statement is an apt encapsulation of the agenda spearheaded by the BJP and its Hindu fundamentalist allies to jettison India's constitution authored by Dalit figurehead Dr Bhim Rao Ambedkar and establish a Hindu *rashtra* (nation). Teltumbde, the grandson-in-law of Dr Ambedkar and a vociferous critic of Narendra Modi and the BJP, is one of 16 individuals arrested by the National Investigation Agency (NIA) and imprisoned arbitrarily without trial on fabricated charges of instigating caste-violence and sedition in the 2018 Bhima Koregaon case.

Mirroring the aforementioned real life scenarios, several Indie films portray the disproportionate police brutality and injustice meted out by the Indian legal system to vulnerable Dalits. For instance, *Court* depicts a Dalit political activist Narayan Kamble (Vira Sathidar) who is accused of performing seditious songs and dragged subsequently into an unending and bureaucratic court trial with no real hope of bona fide justice. Similarly, Tamil film *Visaranai* (2015) explores the suspension of all human rights in the spatio-carceral precincts of the Indian police station where four Dalit Tamil migrants are arrested on falsified charges, imprisoned and tortured. *Seththumaan/Pig* (2020) by Dalit director Thamizh is based on eminent writer Perumal Murugan's short story delving into the caste politics of meat consumption particularly relatable to the banning of beef consumption by the BJP government in several Indian states. Dalit filmmaker Vinod Kamble's *Kastoori/The Musk* (2019) grapples with the true-life story of a Dalit teenager having to resort to manual scavenging to fund his education. A spectrum of regional-language films *Perariyathavar* and *Veyilmarangal*

(Bijukumar Damodaran, 2014, 2019), *Kammatipaadam* (Rajeev Ravi, 2016), *Chamm* (Rajeev Kumar, 2017), *Asuran* (Vetrimaaran, 2019) and *Palasa 1978* (Karuna Kumar, 2020), Leena Manimekalai's female-focused *Maadathy: An Unfairy Tale* (2019) and T. J. Gnanavel's *Jai Bhim* (2021) endorse the thesis of new wave Dalit cinema (Firstpost.com, 2020).

The film examples in this section foreground the potential to focalise particular Dalit theoretical and conceptual frameworks whilst engaging simultaneously with intersectional filmic and factual discourses of gender, sexuality, caste identity and politics.

Indian philosophical approaches

The expansive constellation of Indian philosophy spans several millennia, but there is potential to identity suitable indigenous epistemologies and philosophical frameworks that could augment the scholarly analysis of Indian Indies. Rasa theory is a template whose provenance is the ancient Hindu religious treatise on drama – the Natyashastra. Rasa aims to compartmentalise visual performance into nine archetypical emotions. Rasa has been privileged as an autochthonous reference point to interpret visual codes and the grammar of Bollywood films. However, the limitations of rasa are the concept's association with 'upper-caste' Brahmin Hinduism and also the reductionist and restrictive property of its nine parameters. The bias towards affect-based expressionism may suit the exaggerated, theatrical and melodramatic mode of Bollywood thematically and performatively, but rasa theory falls short when applied as a theoretical prism to interpret the politically interrogative, radically rational, verisimilar aesthetic and fluid experimentation that differentiates the Indies from Bollywood.

Essentially, the Indies' postmodern agglomeration of form, style and divergent content resists deterministic and essentialising categorisation. The subversive proclivities of several Indie films that challenge the established order and social status quo entail that they do not conform to a fixed paradigm that typifies the formulaic mould of Bollywood blockbusters. Therefore, rasa theory with its religious roots and emotion-centrism may not be the best fit to investigate politically disputatious and iconoclastic independent films which seek to disrupt rather than adhere to predetermined systems, structures and templates.

Ancient Indian Cārvāka philosophy from the Lokāyata tradition is a nihilist *weltanschauung* that predates Nietzsche's own contestation of truth claims, existence of god and logocentrism. Iconoclastic and non-conformist, the Cārvāka school of thought confronted religious orthodoxy and exclusivity in its emergence as the 'lone contender against the pro-Vedic Brahmanical schools' as well as the 'non-Vedic Buddhist and Jain schools' (Bhattacharya, 2011, p. 9). The atheist Cārvākas did not subscribe to belief in an afterlife, rebirth or the soul outliving the corporeal form after death. Cārvākas endorsed an Epicurean lifestyle encouraging enjoyment of worldly pleasures. The Cārvāka credo is invoked and interpreted directly in *Ship of Theseus* through a character strategically named Carvaka (Vinay Shukla) who engages in a Socratic duel with a Jain monk Maitreya (Neeraj Kabi) who subscribes to a more metaphysical philosophy of spiritual existence. In another Indie film example, the hedonistic and nihilistic eponymous character in the film *Gandu/Asshole* embodies the Cārvāka ethos of libidinal pleasures. In terms of a suitable analytical touchstone to interpret the postmodern nihilism of *Gandu*, Cārvāka philosophy presents a more carnivalesque and indigenous conceptual alternative to canonical yet time-worn western psychoanalytical paradigms such as Freudian developmental stages, drives and impulses.

Anil Kumar Sarkar (1987) explores non-Vedic systems outside the dominant Hindu Vedic canon, exploring Cārvāka, Jain and Buddhist philosophical frameworks. *Mukti Bhawan/Hotel Salvation* engages with the Hindu quest for the soul to find liberation or *moksha* (salvation) in the afterlife presenting themes such as karma, filial duty, worldly and human bonds, desire and renunciation of material existence – concepts that coexist in Hindu, Buddhist and Jain philosophies. Gopalan Mullick's *Explorations in Cinema Through Classical Indian Theories* (2020) presents an array of indigenous and hybrid Indian and western theoretical concepts on visual aesthetics and art including a cross-epistemological comparative evaluation of film genre through classical Indian Nyaya theory and French philosopher Jacques Lacan's ideas on signification. Overall, innovative and intrepid deployment of radical Indian philosophical paradigms could help in the formulation of culturally attuned, textured and granular critical readings of philosophically oriented Indian Indie films.

Conclusion

The strong thrust towards decolonising the curriculum in western universities is accompanied by the need to decentralise Eurocentric scholarly paradigms and histories of cinema. A more pluralistic playing field involving scholarly perspectives and discursive narratives from on the ground in the Global South is therefore essential. In this regard, the new Indies' glocal form and style calls for a simultaneously contextualised yet broader representative theoretical and philosophical toolkit which would be apposite to this glocal postmodern film form that coalesces the local and global.

Generation of new perspectives and fresh conceptual frameworks whilst recasting, recontextualising and building on existing paradigms would be a favourable direction of travel in the scholarly investigation of new independent Indian cinema.

References

Althusser, L. (1972). Ideology and ideological state apparatuses (Notes towards an investigation). In: *Lenin and philosophy and other essays*. New York: Monthly Review, pp. 85–126.

Appadurai, A. (1996). *Modernity at large: Cultural dimensions of globalization*. Minnesota: University of Minnesota Press.

Barthes, R. (1981). *Camera lucida: Reflections on photography*. New York: Hill & Wang.

Bhan, G. (2019). Notes on a Southern urban practice. *Environment & Urbanization*, 31(2), pp. 639–654.

Bhattacharya, R. (2011). *Studies on the Cārvāka/ Lokāyata*. London: Anthem Press.

Brooks, A. (1997). *Postfeminisms*. Oxon: Routledge.

Butler, J. (1990). *Gender trouble: Feminism and the subversion of identity*. Abingdon: Routledge.

Caldwell, J. (2008). *Production culture*. Durham, NC: Duke University Press.

Dasgupta, R. (2017). *Digital queer cultures in India: Politics, intimacies and belonging*. Oxon: Routledge.

Devasundaram, A. (2016a). Bollywood's soft power: Branding the nation, sustaining a meta-hegemony. In: P. Cooke, ed., *Soft power, film culture and the BRICS, new cinemas journal of contemporary film*. Intellect, 14(1), pp. 51–70.

Devasundaram, A. (2016b). *India's new independent cinema: Rise of the hybrid*. New York: Routledge.

Devasundaram, A. (2017). Alternative narratives from new Indian indie cinema. *Asia Dialogue*. [online] Available at: https://theasiadialogue.com/2017/07/25/alternative-narratives-from-new-indian-indie-cinema/ [Accessed 20 Aug. 2021].

Devasundaram, A. (2018). Beyond brand Bollywood: Alternative articulations of geopolitical discourse in New Indian Films. In: R. Saunders and V. Strukov, eds., *Popular geopolitics: Plotting an evolving interdiscipline*. Oxon: Routledge, pp. 152–173.

Devasundaram, A. (2020a). Subalterns and the city: Dubai as cross-cultural caravanserai in City of life and Pinky Memsaab. *Transnational screens*. Routledge. 11(3), 248–265, DOI: 10.1080/25785273.2020.1823077

Devasundaram, A. (2020b). Interrogating patriarchy: Transgressive discourses of "F-Rated" independent Hindi films. *BioScope: South Asian Screen Studies*, 11(1), pp. 27–43.

Devasundaram, A. (2021). *Framing police-related urban violence: Cinematic crosscurrents from the global south*. Urban Violence, British Academy. www.thebritishacademy.ac.uk/documents/3340/Urban-Violence.pdf.

Devasundaram, A. (forthcoming in 2022). Local realism, Indian independent film as a socio-political medium. In: A. Taha and D. Menon, eds., *Cinemas of the global south: Towards a new aesthetics*. New York: Routledge.

Dudrah, R. (2012). *Bollywood travels*. Oxon: Routledge.

The Express Tribune. (2020). Bollywood goes digital: New Indian films to release online | The Express Tribune. [online] Available at: https://tribune.com. pk/story/2222005/bollywood-goes-digital-new-indian-films-release-online [Accessed 21 Aug. 2021].

Fanon, F. (1963). *The wretched of the earth*. New York: Grove Weidenfeld.

Firstpost. (2020). *Dalitprotagonists – Firstpost*. [online] Available at: www.first post.com/tag/dalitprotagonists [Accessed 23 Aug. 2021].

Foucault, M. (1978). *The history of sexuality: Volume one*. New York: Vintage Books.

Foucault, M. (1986). Of other spaces, Trans. Jay Miskowiec. *Diacritics*, 16(1), Spring, pp. 22–27.

Hagener, M., Hediger, V. and Strohmaier, A. (2016). *The state of post-cinema*. London: Palgrave Macmillan.

Harvey, D. (2012). *Rebel cities*. London: Verso.

Lefebvre, H. (1991). *The production of space*. Oxon: Blackwell.

Mehta, S. (2019). Precarity and new media: Through the lens of Indian creators. *International Journal of Communication*, 13, pp. 5548–5567.

Mishra, S. (2021). Misogyny and erotic pleasure in Bollywood's "item numbers". In: G. Fosbraey and N. Puckey, eds., *Misogyny, toxic masculinity and heteronormativity in post-2000 popular music*. Cham, Switzerland: Palgrave Macmillan, pp. 55–72.

Mullick, G. (2021). *Explorations in cinema through classical Indian theories*. Cham, Switzerland: Palgrave Macmillan.

Mulvey, L. (1975). Visual pleasure and narrative cinema. *Screen*, 16(3), pp. 6–18.

Nandy, A. (1998). *The secret politics of our desires*. London: Zed Books.

Narayan, U. (1998). Essence of culture and a sense of history: A feminist critique of cultural essentialism. *Hypatia*, 13(2), pp. 86–106.

Narine, N. (2010). Global trauma and the cinematic network society. *Critical Studies in Media Communication*, 27(3), pp. 209–234.

Nye, J. (1990). *Bound to lead: The changing nature of American power*. London: Basic Books.

PWC/ASSOCHAM. (2018). *Video on demand: Entertainment reimagined*. [online] Available at: www.pwc.in/assets/pdfs/publications/2018/video-on-demand.pdf [Accessed 23 Aug. 2021].

Rai, A. (2019). *Jugaad time: Ecologies of everyday hacking in India*. Durham: Duke University Press.

Roy, A. (2011). Slumdog cities: Rethinking subaltern urbanism. *International Journal of Urban and Regional Research*, 35(2), pp. 223–238.

Sarkar, A. (1987). *Dynamic facets of Indian thought: Three Non-Vedic systems: 2*. New Delhi: South Asia Books.

Spivak, G. (1994). Can the subaltern speak? In: P. Williams and L. Chrisman, eds., *Colonial discourse and post-colonial theory*. New York: Columbia University Press, pp. 66–111.

Teltumbde, A. (2017). *Dalits: Past, present and future*. Oxon: Routledge.

Thussu, D. (2013). *Communicating India's soft power: Buddha to Bollywood*. New York: Palgrave Macmillan.

Wilkerson, I. (2021). *Caste: The origins of our discontents*. Waterville, Maine: Cengage Gale.

Yengde, S. (2018). Dalit cinema. *South Asia: Journal of South Asian Studies*, 41(3), pp. 503–518.

Yengde, S. (2019). *Caste matters*. Gurgaon: Penguin Viking.

5 From multiplex to Netflix
Indie funding, distribution and exhibition

Overview

In the early stages of their journey around 2010, alternative Indian films relied largely on exhibition in cinema multiplexes integrated into shopping complexes – *malltiplexes* (Rai, 2009) – which burgeoned in Indian cosmopolitan centres concomitant with the nation's free market liberalisation. In the new millennium, these multiscreen venues had started to replace traditional stand-alone cinema halls (Athique and Hill, 2010).

Alongside limited channels of exhibition and distribution, films made outside the dominant Bollywood studio system were often dependent on the limited funding resources of the National Film Development Corporation (NFDC). The NFDC played a prominent role during the halcyon days of the new wave Parallel cinema movement in the 1970s and '80s. The organisation's influence and reach started to wane with the entry of the Rupert Murdoch-owned STAR TV satellite television network in the early 1990s, which also wrested control of the airwaves from India's solitary state-run terrestrial TV channel Doordarshan. During India's socialist era in the 1980s, Doordarshan was a one-stop national conduit for news, entertainment, education and NFDC-produced films which were showcased on the national channel to a pan-Indian viewership.

Since the emergence of the independent Indian new wave in 2010, there has been a demonstrable paradigm shift in viewer attitudes to unconventional film content. Over a decade, audiences in major Indian cities and smaller towns have developed an appetite for a varied cinematic diet that traverses mainstream and independent, national and global visual media. Much of this diversification in the audience palette is attributable to expanded exposure and wider access to eclectic films through cable television, torrent downloads, film festivals and the entry of Netflix and Amazon Prime Video into the Indian market in 2016. The increasing visibility and success of new independent Indian films across a range of platforms is therefore interlinked

DOI: 10.4324/9781003089001-6

with the growing cinematic consciousness and sense of experimentation amongst Indian audiences. Philosophically and intellectually incisive films such as *Ship of Theseus* gaining multiplex screening space in India's smaller Y (Tier-2) and Z (Tier-3) category cities and towns exemplifies the transformation in patterns of audience consumption, although this trend is prevalent largely amongst the middle-class demographic.

In relation to funding, exhibition and distribution opportunities, the assorted spectrum and hierarchised levels of Indian Indies (mentioned in Chapter 1) comes into play. Indies that benefit from alliances with big corporate production houses and established funders and distributors have tended to gain greater visibility and likelihood of success. On the other hand, low-profile first-time filmmakers are often compelled to self-fund their projects as reflected in the perspective of debut directors Vishal Mourya and Debi Prasad Lenka in relation to their film *B For Bundelkhand* (2020) which charts the predicament of impoverished farmers in the film's titular rural region. The directors state:

> Finance and distribution are like a nightmare for new filmmakers. New filmmakers have innovative ideas, good stories, a good team but no finance and selling plan. The real issue is nobody believes in you until you make your first feature film. All the big production houses prefer star value rather than good content.
>
> (Srivastava, 2021)

As an alternative to hitherto dominant mainstream conduits of exhibition such as urban multiplexes, film festivals, both in India and overseas, continue to serve as a lifeline for Indie film exhibition. Across 2010–21, bespoke Indian and South Asian film festivals such as the UK Asian Film Festival (UKAFF), New Generations Independent Indian Film Festival Frankfurt and Indian Film Festival of Los Angeles (IFFLA) in western countries have championed new Indian Indie cinema, showcasing latest releases and curating conversations around radical changes generated by this new form of Indian cinema. Across India, Indie-focused film festivals in regions such as Dharamshala, Odisha, Kerala and Ladakh epitomise the increasingly diffuse geographical spread of film festivals across the country.

The most significant and indeed monumental metamorphosis that has transpired in relation to Indian Indie exhibition and distribution is the advent of Netflix and Amazon Prime Video in 2016. The two web streaming leviathans in addition to several indigenous varieties, referred to in India as OTT (over-the-top) platforms, have in significant measure filled the vacuum of an absent independent filmmaking infrastructure by providing a digital, demotic, regionally and globally accessible portal of exhibition and distribution.

The next sections will explore the various channels of funding, distribution and exhibition from the point of view of new independent Indian cinema.

Multiplexes

The terrain of Indian multiscreen exhibition has largely been spearheaded by the PVR Cinemas chain which was established in 1995 concomitant with India's free market liberalisation and the eventual decentralisation of standalone single-screen cinemas. The commercial possibilities of multiscreen venues incepted into shopping complexes became a template that folded into India's neoliberal turn towards consumer culture. Since the 2000s, the PVR franchise has witnessed the emergence of competitors such as INOX Leisure Ltd, Cinepolis India, Carnival Cinemas and SRS Cinemas. The tally in India of 925 screens in 2009 magnified to 3200 multiplex screens in 2019 (Statista.com, 2021). This exponential growth of multiplexes is indicative of a general trend of widening accessibility to visual media in India although 2020 bucked the trend with significantly diminished footfall in multiplexes owing to the Covid-19 pandemic. Whilst multiplex cinemas have gradually started to acknowledge the viability of new Indian Indie films, particularly since the critical acclaim and commercial success garnered by films such as *Ship of Theseus* and *The Lunchbox* in 2013, it was a different scenario in the first decade of the 2000s when multiplexes started to supplant traditional standalone cinema halls.

During their incipient stage, around the start of the new millennium, multiplexes were independent filmmakers' new hope for a more pluralistic platform to showcase lower-budget alternative films in a Bollywood-dominated terrain. This optimistic vision proved premature, and disillusionment took root when it became evident that multiscreen cinemas analogous to their single-screen predecessors favoured lucrative and box-office-friendly Bollywood blockbusters over unconventional film content. In effect, Bollywood's monopoly extended to the multiplex sector where blockbusters were deemed more financially viable and therefore screening schedules were occupied invariably and disproportionately by popular Bollywood films. Indie films with topical or polemic content were relegated to an esoteric strand appropriately titled Director's Rare. Films screened under the Director's Rare banner were sporadic and scheduled inconveniently during working weekdays at mid-afternoon time slots that were not conducive to a broader audience. Moreover, multiplex ticket pricing for low-budget Indie films was on par with Bollywood blockbusters, rendering Indie films out of the reach of low-income sections of the population, particularly students. The increasing box-office viability of independent films including obscure yet unexpectedly popular productions such as Kenny Basumatary's Assamese film *Local Kung Fu* (2013) made on a budget of Rupees 95,000 (around £1000) gained a nationwide release and sufficient success to spawn a sequel in 2017. An expanding portfolio of more high-profile indies such as *Lipstick Under My Burkha* alerted the multiplexes to the increasing potential and pulling power of new Indies. However, for every independent Indian film that makes it to multiplex screens, there are several others that are rejected and often depend on the film festival circuit or streaming platforms such as Netflix, Amazon Prime Video and MUBI for exhibition. Examples include 'fiercely indie films' (Chatterjee, 2018) such as *Jonaki/Firefly* (Aditya Vikram Sengupta, 2018), *Ma'Ama* (Dominic Sangma, 2018), *Bhonsle* (Devashish Makhija, 2018) and *Ghode Ko Jalebi Khilane Le Ja Riya Hoon/ Taking the Horse to Eat Jalebis* (Anamika Haksar, 2019).

National Film Development Corporation (NFDC)

The National Film Development Corporation was established in 1980 from a merger between the Film Finance Corporation (FFC) founded in 1960 and the Indian Motion Pictures Export Corporation (IMPEC). Under the aegis of the FFC/NFDC, the Indian government patronised new wave Parallel cinema of the 1970s and '80s and its engagement with social realist state of the nation stories. This policy towards arthouse cinema seems antithetical to the contemporary neoliberal orientation of successive post-liberalisation Indian governments since the 1990s which have aligned with and sanctioned the lucrative and popular Bollywood industry as the dominant cultural emissary of Indian cultural soft power (see Chapter 4). With the rise of subscription television networks, entry of multinational film production corporations and increased privatisation in the 1990s, the centrality of NFDC was denuded and the organisation faced an existential crisis. The elemental question for the NFDC pivoted on rebranding and refurbishing its approach as the Corporation endeavoured to reiterate its relevance and raison d'etre in the digital age. Sudha Tiwari (2018, p. 25) charts the evolutionary trajectory of NFDC, asserting that the organisation has come 'full circle' in terms of its support for Parallel cinema auteur Mani Kaul's arthouse magnum opus *Uski Roti* in 1970 which 'hardly got any theatrical release' and Ritesh Batra's independent film *The Lunchbox* which gained global commercial success in 2013.

NFDC initiatives such as Film Bazaar have been particularly conspicuous in presenting an international platform in the form of a film co-production and distribution market to assist the proliferation of Indian Indies. The NFDC Film Bazaar is held concomitant with the annual International Film Festival of India (IFFI) in Goa. During the Covid-19 pandemic in 2020, Film Bazaar utilised its virtual interface and online Viewing Room (VR) where global producers, distribution companies and film festivals could gain online access to an extensive catalogue of NFDC-funded or co-produced films recently completed or in the final stage of editing and post-production. A subset of the Film Bazaar is the Work-in-Progress (WIP) Lab which provides selected filmmakers the opportunity to screen rough cuts of their films to a panel of renowned international mentors and gain advice and feedback. Notable WIP projects include *I Am Kalam* (2010), *Miss Lovely*, *Ship of Theseus*, *B.A. Pass* (all 2012) and *Margarita With a Straw* (2015) (Tiwari, 2018, p. 37). One of the limitations of the WIP initiative is its selectivity – only five films are earmarked for the scheme which is insubstantial considering the sheer volume of filmmaking output in India.

NFDC Screenwriters' Lab is another annual initiative to help screenwriters develop screenplay drafts with guidance from reputed international mentors in one-on-one sessions. Master classes, lectures and short workshops on structure, character development, dialogue, scene writing, visual codes and synopsis writing are integrated into the Lab (Filmbazaarindia.com, 2021). The scheme also presents a forum to pitch film projects to Indian and global producers and funders. This initiative has spawned several notable Indian Indies including *Lipstick Under My Burkha*, *The Lunchbox*, *Titli*, *Chauranga* and *The Good Road*. Once again, the restricted number of projects selected for the Lab is conspicuous in a contemporary scenario where there is a plenitude of independent films from emerging filmmakers.

The India Pavilion hosted by the National Film Development Corporation (NFDC) and the Ministry of Information and Broadcasting (MIB) at the Cannes Film Market and at the Berlin International Film Festival is an important resource for the Indian contingent of actors, producers and film programmers. In 2017, Nandita Das utilised this forum to promote her film *Manto* about the iconic short story writer Saadat Hasan Manto to prospective buyers and distributors at Cannes.

In an attempt to contemporise its operational format and branding, NFDC introduced its own web streaming subscription platform NFDC Cinemas of India featuring an assortment of iconic post-independence arthouse and new wave Parallel films in addition to an array of contemporary new Indian Indie films. Akin to the Central Board of Film Certification (CBFC) the NFDC is presided over by the Ministry of Information and Broadcasting which lends a political dimension to the organisation's role, function and appointment of executive positions. In 2020, the central government announced the merger of NFDC with four government film and media units including

Films Division, the Directorate of Film Festivals, National Film Archive of India and the Children's Film Society of India.

Overall, the NFDC through its various initiatives extends several national and international avenues for independent filmmakers to ideate, fund and disseminate their films. However, these opportunities can be limited, necessitating a preponderance of excluded filmmakers to seek alternative pathways to funding and distribution.

Crowdfunding

Sourcing financial input from potential audiences to support independent film production has been a mainstay for several new wave Indie filmmakers since Onir adopted global crowdfunding for his film *I Am* (2010) which was facilitated by 400 donors across 45 countries. South Indian director Pawan Kumar followed a similar route with his Kannada film *Lucia* for which he accumulated crowd contributions in just 27 days. Utilising Facebook and weblogs, Kumar mounted a relentless publicity campaign eventually gaining his target budget of Rupees 51 lakhs (around £51,000) through audience contributions (Devasundaram, 2016).

As demonstrated by Kumar's approach to *Lucia*, crowdfunding is a multifaceted and procedural undertaking. It involves identification of a suitable crowdfunding platform, creating a fundraiser announcement containing information about the film project, publicising the fundraiser through social media channels and engagement with donors via incentives and acknowledgement (Dasgupta, 2018).

The first instance of crowdfunding in Indian cinema was Parallel cinema auteur Shyam Bengal's film *Manthan/The Churning* in 1976 which enlisted financial participation of 500,000 dairy farmers in Gujarat who contributed a portion of their daily earnings to become co-producers of the film. Therefore, crowdfunding is another genealogical connecting link between new wave Parallel cinema of the 1970s–'80s and the contemporary new independent Indian films.

The ascendancy of crowdfunding since 2010 has been schematised through local, national and international crowdfunding organisations and online portals including Catapooolt, Kickstarter, Wishberry, GoFundMe, Ketto and Indiegogo. There is a distinct connection between Indie films espousing radical, transgressive, taboo or controversial content and crowdfunding as a mechanism to sidestep the intrusive, restrictive and often oppositional mainstream funding sources such as corporate production houses or the state-influenced NFDC. *Life of an Outcast* (Pawan Shrivastava, 2018) and *Evening Shadows* (Sridhar Rangayan, 2018) whose visceral and realistic portrayals of caste prejudice and homosexuality entailed a struggle for the filmmakers to gain mainstream funding. They therefore turned to audience donations as an alternative resource alongside social media promotion to bring their projects to fruition. In the case of *Evening Shadows*, the film's trailer gained around 50000 views on Facebook and around 9000 views on YouTube from its Indiegogo crowdfunding campaign.

Integrating an advocacy incentive into the campaign, the filmmaker's crowdfunding pitch stated that by supporting *Evening Shadows*, a portion of audience donations would contribute to forming an organised support group for parents of LGBTQ+ people in Mumbai. In general, the intersection between crowdfunded Indian Indie films, advocacy and awareness-generation of social issues such as commercial surrogacy, neoliberalism and LGBTQ+ rights (Mendes, 2018) is a distinctive aspect of several new independent films.

Film festivals

Bespoke Indian and South Asian film festivals in the UK and USA were among the first to acknowledge and embrace the emergence of a new wave of independent Indian cinema around 2010. The UK Asian Film Festival (UKAFF), the longest-running Indian and South Asian cinema showcase outside India, has screened several seminal Indian Indie films spanning the Indies evolutionary cycle, from *Peepli Live* and *I Am* in 2011 and *Aligarh* (2016) to *Raahgir/The Wayfarers* (2019) and *The Great Indian Kitchen* in 2021. The festival's F-Rated theme in 2018 focused on female-centric Indie films including a collaborative screening with the Glasgow Film Festival of Rima Das's *Village Rockstars*. UKAFF marked its 23rd anniversary in 2021 with the theme 'Ray of Hope', commemorating the birth centenary of Satyajit Ray and showcasing contemporary Indian Indies inspired thematically or stylistically by Ray's oeuvre. Over the years, UKAFF has formulated a synergistic relationship with the new Indian and South India independent film sectors by featuring controversial films such as *Lipstick Under My Burkha* which was denied a certificate of release in India and *Zindagi Tamasha* (2021), banned in Pakistan. According to festival founder/ director Dr Pushpinder Chowdhry (2021), 'UKAFF offers a platform especially for young independent filmmakers to introduce their work, discuss the filmmaking process and initiate dialogue among diverse audiences about cutting-edge topics'.

A global conference – Curation During the Time of Covid – was held as part of UKAFF 2021 featuring leading South Asian film festival curators from MAMI Mumbai Film Festival, Diorama, New Generations Independent Indian Film Festival Frankfurt, Australian Film Festival of India, Chicago South Asian Film Festival, Kashish Queer Film Festival and Queer

Asia Film Festival. This pioneering event rendered accessible globally via video (UKAFF, 2021) is the launchpad for UKAFF to establish a federation of South Asian festivals. The main objectives include sharing knowledge, skills, resources and devising strategies to engage with the new post-Covid 19 landscape of hybrid multiplatform film festival delivery whilst working synergistically with web streaming platforms.

In recent years, the tendency for filmmakers to clamour towards formalising 'direct-to-digital' exhibition deals with web platforms at the first opportunity has led to friction with film festivals who often discover that some of their centrepiece films are released on Netflix or Amazon Prime Video either prior to or during festival timelines. The Covid-19 pandemic in 2020–21 has underscored the growing monopoly of streaming giants and kindled the need for the aforementioned symbiotic and strategic agreements and transparent channels of communication between filmmakers, film festivals and dominant web streaming portals.

Reiterating the importance of overseas festivals as a platform to promote new filmmaking voices but also facilitate exhibition of proscribed content, Jayan Cherian's controversial film *Papilio Buddha* which was denied a certificate of release in India by the CBFC was showcased at the Berlinale which consistently features new Indian Indies such as Nagaraj Manjule's *Sairat*, Akshay Indikar's *Sthalpuran/Chronicle of Space* and Chaitanya Tamhane's *The Disciple* in its annual repertoire. The London Indian Film Festival (LIFF) has also been prominent in screening independent Indian films such as *Lucia* which won the Audience Choice Award in 2013. Straddling production, exhibition and distribution, Neeraj Churi, founder of UK-based Lotus Visual Productions explains:

> [The company] was started with the sole purpose of producing and promoting South Asian LGBTQ+ films all over the world. We sponsor the QDrishti Film Grant via the Kashish International Film Festival to help bring LGBTQ+ scripts to screen. We also promote South Asian queer cinema through theatrical screenings and curating films for festivals.
>
> (Churi, 2021)

Monia Acciari's (2019) research on Indian film curation practice locates film festivals as 'counter-archives' that can challenge dominant national histories and hegemonic socio-political metanarratives, with curated films acting as 'channels to reassess the everyday social life of India, and shape a renovated image of the nation'. The counter-narratives of several radical and polemical independent Indian films certainly lend credence to this thesis which demarcates the act of constructing a curatorial assemblage of dissenting film narratives in the crucible of film festivals as building a spatio-temporal arena to present alternative interpretations, raise awareness and articulate resistance.

Indie-focused Indian production companies

During the incipient stages of the independent new wave, the paucity of funding and distribution opportunities precipitated the establishment of autonomous Indie-focused companies such as the erstwhile Phantom Films owned collaboratively by Anurag Kashyap and other filmmakers. Dynamic and versatile independent producers including Guneet Monga set up Sikhya Entertainment and Manish Mundra started Drishyam Films.

Established with the aim to 'rekindle India's independent cinema movement' through 'socially significant, non-escapist narratives' (Menon, 2017), Yoodlee Films, a subset of Indian music label company Saregama (formerly HMV), specialises in independent films with experimental strategies and unconventional storylines. Yoodlee's roster of Indie films includes *Ajji, KD, Noblemen, Chaman Bahar, Music Teacher* and *Hamid*. Siddharth Anand Kumar Vice President of Yoodlee's Film and Television division states:

> there definitely is an audience, between the ages of 18–30, who are yearning to watch flicks like *Lunchbox*, *Haraamkhor* or *Masaan* in theatres, on VOD platforms like Netflix or via major channels like Star Select HD. We just need to balance the supply-demand chain.
>
> (Menon, 2017)

Targeting the aforementioned Indian audience age-range, Yoodlee caters to the ongoing trend of increasingly experimental and expanding viewer tastes. Notably, Yoodlee's catalogue of film productions is multilingual and spans a broad geographical spectrum of regional contexts. For instance, *Abhi and Anu* is a bilingual Tamil/Malayalam film. *KD* is a Tamil film set in the deep south of Tamil Nadu and deals with the arcane practice of senicide – euthanising of elderly parents by their families with a view to acquiring family inheritance. On a different register but equally visceral, Vandana Kataria's *Noblemen* is set in an elite boarding school in the foothills of the Himalayas and grapples with themes of homosexuality and violent bullying.

Alongside this diverse repertoire of alternative content, Yoodlee Films is prolific in terms of production, with an output of 10 films in 15 months and an ambitious target of 'producing 100 films in five to seven years' (Seta, 2018). A facet that distinguishes Yoodlee from other film production companies is that all its personnel are film practitioners from various persuasions – directors, producers, assistant directors and scriptwriters. The company has devised specific standard operating procedures including a stipulation that all filming must be on live locations with synchronised recorded sound rather than dubbed audio which is often used in Bollywood (Seta, 2018).

Yoodlee is versatile in disseminating its productions across multiplexes, film festivals, Netflix and Amazon Prime Video. For example, the visceral rape-revenge saga *Ajji* screened at a plethora of international film festivals including Busan and the UK Asian Film Festival eventually nesting in the online catalogue of Netflix.

Yoodlee's business model aims to facilitate creation of divergent content through comparatively lower levels of investment in film production. This reduces the risk of revenue loss considerably in comparison with big-budget star-studded Bollywood extravaganzas. Lower budgets can also foster the ambitious production output target of 100 independent films prognosticated by Kumar:

> We are being disruptive in how we make films. Now we want to be disruptive in how we distribute films too. . . . We are making films at a budget level which is extremely lower than the big films. So, we need less money to get our returns. If a guy makes a film with Shah Rukh Khan or Salman Khan, he needs to recover Rs 200 crore from the box office otherwise he is in loss. But I don't have such pressure.
>
> (Seta, 2018)

Another Indian company with a bespoke independent film ethos is Drishyam Films which in 2017 earmarked a $20 million production fund to promote the development of independent Indian cinema. The credo articulated by Drishyam Films to 'build a platform for unique voices of Indian independent cinema and create global content with rich Indian flavours' (Drishyamfilms.com, 2021) resonates with the concept of the new Indies as a *glocal* film form. Drishyam has produced an eclectic range of successful independent films including *Ankhon Dekhi* (Rajat Kapoor, 2014), *Waiting* (Anu Menon, 2015) *Masaan* (Neeraj Ghaywan), *Dhanak* (Nagesh Kukunoor, 2015), *Newton* (Amit Masurkar, 2017) and *Rukh* (Atanu Mukherjee, 2017).

In a terrain where new Indian Indies increasingly are looking outward to international co-productions, homegrown companies such as Yoodlee and Drishyam have risen in profile as an important indigenous source of funding, distribution and promotion. Their Indie-focused and artist-oriented approach is distinctive in an encompassing Indian cinema landscape skewed disproportionately towards Bollywood.

International co-productions

Across a decade, independent Indian films increasingly have looked outward to international production houses to co-finance and distribute films with unconventional content and stylistic approaches. International co-productions of Indian Indie films are versatile, involving permutations and combinations of various dimensions including financial/logistical strategic aspects of production/post-production as well as creative and artistic cooperation.

A pertinent example is the futuristic thriller *Manny* (2020) which is an Indo-Latvian co-production with Latvian director Dace Puce and starring Indian actor/co-producer Sonal Sehgal. The film's idiosyncratic storyline focuses on a lesbian Indian author struggling to complete her next book in a writer's retreat in Latvia whilst her Artificial Intelligence operating system 'Manny' takes over management of her life. This hybrid intercultural interpretation of queer identity and gender-based themes in the capsule of a sci-fi thriller alongside allocation of the film's production and post-production processes across India and Latvia typifies the fluid and glocal propensity of new Indian Indie cinema. Similarly, *Kathaah@8* (2019) was publicised as the world's first anthology film in eight Indian languages directed by Singapore-based Indian filmmaker Shilpa Krishnan Shukla.

The Lunchbox – an international co-production involving India's NFDC and Sikhya Entertainment alongside production and distribution companies from France, Germany and USA – was a pathbreaking film which received global recognition and commercial success. International visibility gained by the film provided a platform for director Ritesh Batra to subsequently direct British film *The Sense of an Ending* (2017) and Indian Indie *Photograph* (2019) distributed by Amazon Studios. As international funders become increasingly cognisant of the burgeoning terrain of independent Indian films, avenues for production-oriented financial, infrastructural as well as creative collaboration have become magnified on multifarious levels. Notable in its financial success, *The Lunchbox* gained most of its box-office revenue from non-diasporic international markets outside India (Malvania, 2014).

Vivek Rangachari, producer with Dar Motion Pictures, contextualises the film's overseas profitability:

> I feel the success of this film is due to the global nature of the subject and its beautiful treatment. One of the learnings is that there is a large non-diaspora market ready to accept honest good Indian content. As they say, the more local the content, the more global its appeal.
>
> (Malvania, 2014)

Victor's History (2017) is another interesting example of an international co-production led by Indie-focused Indian production company Yoodlee Films. The film's found-footage premise and handheld camera aesthetic traces the travels in Europe of three male friends from diverse ethnic backgrounds with the unravelling of postcolonial spectres of slavery and exploitation. It is directed by Nicolas Chevaillier who stars in the film alongside the film's co-producer Shoaib Lokhandwala who has been executive and creative producer on several Yoodlee Indie film productions such as *Hamid*, *KD*, *Ascharyachakit!*, *Noblemen*, *Axone* and *Music Teacher*. After exhibition on the global film festival circuit, *Victor's History* was eventually bought by Amazon Prime Video.

In her article *At Home in the World: Co-productions and Indian Alternative Cinema*, Harmanpreet Kaur (2021, pp. 123–124) cites a range of international co-produced Indian Indies including Anup Singh's Indo-European collaborations *Qissa* and *The Song of Scorpions* (2017) alongside *The Lunchbox*, as part of a filmmaking culture that taps international networks for the production, distribution and exhibition of 'locally rooted stories'. This is a throwback to the concept of the Indian Indies as glocal – global in aesthetic and Indian in thematic content (Devasundaram, 2016) – which resonates with Kaur's (2021) identification of the rise of transnational co-production practice in the 'emergence of contemporary alternative cinema in India' (Kaur, 2021). Berlinale Talents is a networking forum that has benefited Indie filmmakers such as Ritesh Batra, Chaitanya Tamhane and Nishtha Jain. CineMart, under the aegis of the International Film Festival of Rotterdam (IFFR), is an international co-production market which along with the Hubert Bals Fund has enabled several independent Indian filmmakers to complete their film projects.

Co-productions are multifaceted and include creative and artistic dimensions as well as strategic funding, production, technical, exhibition and distribution dimensions. For instance, Gustavo Santaolalla, Oscar-winning music composer for *The Motorcycle Diaries* (2004) and *Brokeback Mountain* (2005), scored the music for Kiran Rao's *Dhobi Ghat*. British music composer Andrew T. Mackay composed background music for *Hamid* and *Music Teacher*. Hollywood cinematographer Russell Carpenter (*Titanic*) was DoP and co-executive producer on Leena Yadav's *Parched*, and Kevin Tent (*The Descendants*, *Nebraska*) edited Yadav's film which was produced by Bollywood actor Ajay Devgn. Indo-British music duo Naren Chandavarkar and Benedict Taylor have created music for several Indian Indie films ranging from *Harud*, *Killa* and *Ship of Theseus* to *Newton* and *Sherni*. American composer Wayne Sharpe created music for *Unfreedom* and *Dekh Indian Circus*. Similarly, Ashvin Kumar's *No Fathers in Kashmir* featured

French composers Loik Dury and Christophe 'Disco' Mink who remixed local Kashmiri folk singer Ali Saifuddin's rendition of renowned Kashmiri poet Habba Khatoon's lyrics for the film's soundtrack.

Ritesh Batra's Mumbai-themed *Photograph* involved cinematography by Tim Gillis and Ben Kutchins, editing by John F. Lyons and music by Peter Raeburn. In a similar glocal blend of production and creative collaboration, Alfonso Cuaron acted as executive producer and Polish cinematographer Michal Sobocinski was Director of Photography on Chaitanya Tamhane's Hindustani classical music drama *The Disciple* (2020). Aditya Vikram Sengupta's *Once Upon a Time in Calcutta* (2021) is a France-Norway-India co-production which has as its director of photography Gökhan Tiryaki, cinematographer on Turkish auteur Nuri Bilge Ceylan's *Once Upon a Time in Anatolia* (2011) and *Winter Sleep* (2014).

Torrent downloads

During the formative stages of the new wave, several independent Indian filmmakers acknowledged and credited BitTorrent downloads and filesharing of less accessible global and Indian films with expanding the 'film education' of both filmmakers and film viewers (Devasundaram, 2014, 2016). Anand Gandhi made available online a high-definition version of his film *Ship of Theseus* as a free open-access download after the film had completed its film festival and cinema exhibition cycle. Other filmmakers have raised general concerns about the spectre of lost revenue due to piracy, illegal distribution via torrent networks and leaked film uploads on YouTube and other portals.

Anti-piracy laws and intellectual property rights in India have been fluid and nebulous especially pertaining to the digital domain. The Indian government's proposed draft Cinematograph Amendment Bill 2021 includes a plan to introduce a three-year prison penalty for piracy in the form of unauthorised film recording. The punitive focus has been deemed by the Indian filmmaking community as inadequate or impracticable in terms of preventing film piracy at its structural and foundational roots.

Arguably, the advent of a multitude of web streaming platforms both pay-per-view and subscription has opened a wider window of procurement although income disparity and social class remain factors in relation to audience access. Increasing consumption of visual media via heterodox devices including laptops and mobile phones, enhanced digital connectivity and greater choice of competitive streaming platform subscription rates could potentially diminish the utility of torrent downloads as an informal dissemination mechanism. On the other hand, as explained in the next section, the expansion of Indian state censorship regulations (also see Chapter 3) to include digital OTT streaming portals in its ambit could prompt users to access uncensored versions and uncertified films via alternative online interfaces or return to BitTorrent downloads and filesharing.

Streaming platforms: the rise of Netflix and Amazon Prime Video

As mentioned previously, the entry of subscription web streaming services Netflix and Amazon Prime Video into the Indian market has proved a gamechanger for the Indian Indies. These online platforms have largely filled the vacuum of an absent independent film production ecosystem in the Indian Indie terrain and in significant measure alleviated the independent sector's erstwhile reliance on cinema multiplexes, television channels and DVD distribution. Netflix and Amazon Prime have not only provided production investment for original films and web series but also opened retrospectively a global exhibition window for several low-budget Indies made from 2010 onward. A comprehensive range of seminal Indie films spanning *Gandu, Peepli Live, Dhobi Ghat* and *The Lunchbox* are available alongside newer Indie releases such as *Anarkali of Aarah, Bulbul, Axone* and *Sherni*.

A 2020 Federation of Indian Chambers of Commerce and Industry (FICCI) report takes note of this paradigm shift towards the digital domain and 'direct-to-digital debuts':

> Several film makers released small and low budget films directly on OTT platforms – we estimate over 50 such films in 2019. Unlike in previous years when factors such as unviable marketing, promotion and distribution costs, unavailability of distributors/scepticism on recovery of distribution costs, inappropriate content, etc. lead to a film landing on OTT platforms, films such as Chopstick, House Arrest, Soni, etc. were created specifically for direct release on OTT platforms.
>
> (FICCI.in, 2020)

In this context, Jitender Kumar, Ashish Gupta and Sweta Dixit (2020) present an in-depth statistical appraisal of OTT web platforms in India. There is a gamut of over 40 local, national and international streaming platforms available in India. Acquired from 21st Century Fox in 2019, Disney+ Hotstar alongside its international corporate competitors Netflix and Amazon Prime Video vies for market share with Indian platforms such as Zee5, SonyLIV, Voot, Eros Now, ALT Balaji, Hoichoi and Adda Times. The subscription fee for Netflix is considerably higher at around Rupees 500 (£5) per month compared to Rupees 49 (around £0.50) for Indian channels such as Eros Now (Kumar, Gupta and Dixit, 2020, pp. 9–10). Mirroring a global trend during the Covid-19 pandemic in 2020–21, Netflix and Amazon Prime Video have emerged as dominant players in the Indian market.

India's OTT video market is forecasted to grow from $1.5 billion in 2021 to $12.5 billion in 2030 with expansion expected to emerge from tier II, III and IV cities and towns (Times of India, 2021). This presaged widening of subscription video-on-demand portals is attributable to increasing access to better networks, digital connectivity and smartphones. The content libraries of Netflix and Amazon Prime Video featuring an expansive range of new Indies therefore permits extrapolation of proportional growth in access to new independent Indian cinema both within the country and overseas.

Reflecting the Indie-focused ethos of indigenous production and distribution companies such as Yoodlee and Drishyam but from a web streaming OTT platform standpoint, Gaurav Raturi and Rupinder Kaur established Cinemapreneur – a pay-per-view streaming platform dedicated to films rejected or overlooked by Netflix and Amazon Prime Video (Ghosh, 2020). Unlike the subscription format followed by their more established international counterparts Netflix and Amazon Prime Video, Cinemapreneur charges per film, presenting a more granular, personalised and economical window for viewers to access lesser-known independent films. Highlighting the selectivity of NFDC Film Bazaar and global web streaming platforms, Raturi delineates the function of Cinemapreneur as an additional arena of visibility and a provider of film festival afterlife for small-budget low-profile Indie films:

> At a film bazaar, if 300 films come, 15 get a theatrical release, 10 go to Netflix, five to Amazon, so what happens to the rest? The idea is to celebrate festivals as soon as they end by bringing some of those films to those who can't go there.
>
> (Ghosh, 2020)

In a notable case scenario, Jeo Baby's Malayalam film *The Great Indian Kitchen* (2021) was rejected both by Netflix and Amazon Prime Video. The film gained a regional audience in Kerala through local streaming platform Neestream which ultimately snowballed into the film gaining national and global attention, press publicity and laudatory fan reviews for its trenchant female-driven critique of oppressive domestic and socio-religious patriarchy. This amplified recognition prompted Amazon Prime Video to reverse its previous assessment of the film not 'fitting their criteria' with the platform acquiring and adding *The Great Indian Kitchen* to its catalogue (Vats, 2021).

In essence, smaller and local OTT initiatives devoted to esoteric and low-budget experimental Indies are likely to play an important role considering the market-driven profit-oriented corporate logic of the international web streaming giants which leads them inevitably to the lucrative portals of mainstream Bollywood. Netflix has ratified new deals with Bollywood including a long-term contract with Bollywood producer Karan Johar's Dharmatic Entertainment and a similar agreement with film star Shah Rukh Khan's Red Chillies Entertainment. Netflix's formalised alignment with Bollywood therefore augurs potential replication of the struggle for space the Indies had to contend with previously in the multiplex domain. It remains to be seen whether Bollywood will transplant its meta-hegemonic monopoly of Indian cinemas to the digital domain of Netflix and Amazon Prime Video. For Indian Indie filmmakers who are able to strike deals with global streaming platforms, the benefits far outweigh the travails of pursuing conventional distribution conduits in India.

Highlighting the perennial struggle to gain a theatrical release for small-budget Indian independent films whilst citing the context of his film *Brij Mohan Amar Rahe/Long Live Brij Mohan!* (2018), director Nikhil Bhat demarcates as a preferable alternative to cinema releases the global reach, accessibility and logistical fluidity of digital streaming portals:

> You have to make sure there are no big releases in the weeks before and after your film, the timing has to be correct and the project has to be given its due marketing even though theatrical audience is limited. Netflix, on the other hand, took our film to 190 countries which was the best thing that could have happened to it.
>
> (Jha, 2018)

Crucially, until 2021, Netflix and Amazon have utilised a legislative loophole that excluded internet-based media in India from state regulation to evade censorship norms mandatory for all cinema releases. Whilst conservative Indian audiences have favoured monitoring and redaction of film content, the exemption of web-based film exhibition in India has been a lifeline for progressive and liberal-minded filmmakers and viewers alike: 'A number of users wrote that they loved the content and the Netflix experience, especially the lack of censorship. One user wrote, "Thank you . . . Netflix, our Lord and Savior from censored butchered content"' (Lobato, 2019, p. 124). Online portals' circumvention of draconian state-controlled censorship practices of the CBFC has thus far facilitated a wider range of Indie film content on digital OTT platforms. Controversial and explicit films such as *Gandu* and *Garbage* (2018) and politically critical web series such as *Sacred Games* (2018), *Leila* (2019) and *Paatal Lok/Netherworld* (2020) have been offered in their uncut avatars to Indian and global audiences. This relative creative freedom of the online domain presented an impetus for filmmakers to craft their films specifically for the digital space rather than plough through the conventional CBFC censorship-ridden obstacle course towards conventional cinema screenings. This was the case till the BJP government, in a significant unilateral directive, introduced sweeping new regulations in 2020–21 expanding the ambit of censorship to include web streaming platforms. Under the new rules, online films, digital news and current affairs content were all brought under the control of the Ministry of Information and Broadcasting. The state's executive order entails streaming platforms such as Netflix, Amazon Prime Video and Disney+ Hotstar would effectively be governed by the I&B Ministry.

Ministry sources justified the order with the following statement:

> simply bringing 'content' from under the purview of IT to I&B. OTT though is a new platform, where concern against content couldn't be raised with government earlier, which will now be possible. I&B now will be the nodal ministry.
>
> (Saha, 2020)

Whilst Netflix and Amazon Prime continue to develop web series, commission original independent feature films and add films to their catalogues, it is conceivable that the intervention of the state through regulation and censorship will influence the level of autonomy, acceptance and proliferation of Indian Indie films on these global platforms. This is particularly applicable to Indie films containing content that does not comply with the ruling order and censoring authorities' prescribed parameters, diktats, political, moral and religious codes.

References

Acciari, M. (2019). The permanency of film festivals: Archiving the changing India. *South Asian Film and Media Journal*, 10(1), pp. 41–57.

Athique, A. and Hill, D. (2010). *The multiplex in India: A cultural economy of urban leisure*. Oxon: Routledge.

Chatterjee, S. (2018). 5 Indian films that pushed indie cinema boundaries in 2018. *NDTV.com*. [online] Available at: www.ndtv.com/entertainment/yearender-2018-five-indian-films-that-pushed-indie-cinema-boundaries-this-year-1970035 [Accessed 31 July 2021].

Chowdhry, P. (2021), [personal communication]. 30 Aug. 2021.

Churi, N. (2021), [personal communication]. 1 Sep. 2021.

Dasgupta, S. (2018). How crowdfunding in films works in India – Media India group. *Media India Group.* [online] Available at: https://mediaindia.eu/cinema/how-crowdfunding-in-films-works-in-india/ [Accessed 6 Aug. 2021].

Devasundaram, A. (2014). Cyber buccaneers, public and pirate spheres: The phenomenon of BitTorrent downloads in the transforming terrain of Indian cinema. *Media International Australia*, 152, pp. 108–118.

Devasundaram, A. (2016). *India's new independent cinema: Rise of the hybrid.* New York: Routledge.

Drishyamfilms.com. (2021). *About Us – Drishyam films.* [online] Available at: www.drishyamfilms.com/about-us/ [Accessed 1 Aug. 2021].

FICCI.in. (2020). *The era of consumer A.R.T. March 2020 India's media & entertainment sector.* [online] Available at: https://ficci.in/spdocument/23200/FICCI-EY-Report-media-and-entertainment-2020.pdf [Accessed 13 Aug. 2021].

Filmbazaarindia.com. (2021). [online] Available at: https://filmbazaarindia.com/pdf/2021/swl/swlfaq2021.pdf [Accessed 3 Aug. 2021].

Ghosh, T. (2020). Cinemapreneur, a new OTT platform, is solely dedicated to Indian indie films. *The Indian Express.* [online] Available at: https://indianexpress.com/article/entertainment/web-series/cinemapreneur-a-new-ott-platform-is-solely-dedicated-to-indian-indie-films-6553331/ [Accessed 13 Aug. 2021].

Jha, L. (2018). Indian filmmakers go digital for small movies. mint. [online] Available at: www.livemint.com/Consumer/iMAmWFcqXU0Opl1rGBNroN/Indian-filmmakers-go-digital-for-small-movies.html [Accessed 6 Aug. 2021].

Kaur, H. (2021). At home in the world: Co-productions and Indian alternative cinema. *BioScope* 11(2), SAGE, pp. 123–145.

Kumar, J., Gupta, A. and Dixit, S. (2020). Netflix: SVoD entertainment of next gen. *Emerald Emerging Markets Case Studies*, 10(3), pp. 1–36.

Malvania, U. (2014). The Lunchbox: Simple fare proves the right recipe for global box-office success. *Business Standard India.* 10 Apr. [online] Available at: www.business-standard.com/article/companies/the-lunchbox-simple-fare-proves-the-right-recipe-for-global-box-office-success-114041000139_1.html [Accessed 27 Aug. 2021].

Mendes, A. (2018). Indie crowdfunded narratives of commercial surrogacy, or the contested bodies of neoliberalism: Onir's *I Am Afia* and Arpita Kumar's *Sita*. In: A. Devasundaram, ed., *Indian cinema beyond Bollywood: The new independent cinema revolution.* New York: Routledge.

Menon, A. (2017). Yoodlee films intends to rekindle India's independent cinema movement. *Indulgexpress.com.* [online] Available at: www.indulgexpress.com/entertainment/cinema/2017/jul/28/yoodlee-films-intends-to-rekindle-indias-independent-cinema-movement-2872.html [Accessed 1 Aug. 2021].

Rai, A. (2009). *Untimely Bollywood.* New York: Duke University Press.

Saha, P. (2020). Streaming platforms, digital news brought under I&B ministry, says govt order. *India Today.* [online] Available at: www.indiatoday.in/india/story/streaming-platforms-digital-news-under-centre-1739974-2020-11-11 [Accessed 3 Aug. 2021].

Seta, K. (2018). We treat filmmakers as partners, not vendors: Siddharth Anand Kumar of Yoodlee Films. *Cinestaan*. [online] Available at: www.cinestaan.com/articles/2018/may/5/12984 [Accessed 1 Aug. 2021].

Srivastava, K. (2021). *Indianfilminstitute.org*. [online] Available at: www.indian filminstitute.org/post/how-i-made-it-b-for-bundelkhand-2020 [Accessed 6 Aug. 2021].

Statista.com. (2021). *India: Number of multiplex screens | Statista*. [online] Available at: www.statista.com/statistics/731215/number-of-multiplex-theatres-india/ [Accessed 6 Aug. 2021].

Times of India. (2021). India's video OTT market to touch $12.5 bn by 2030. *The Times of India*. [online] Available at: https://timesofindia.indiatimes.com/busi ness/india-business/indias-video-ott-market-to-touch-12-5-bn-by-2030-report/ articleshow/84517492.cms [Accessed 5 Aug. 2021].

Tiwari, S. (2018). From new cinema to new indie cinema: The story of NFDC and Film Bazaar. In: A. Devasundaram, ed., *Indian cinema beyond Bollywood: The new independent cinema revolution*. New York: Routledge, pp. 25–45.

UKAFF 2021. (2021). *International South Asian film festival conference*. [online] Available at: www.tonguesonfire.com/video/international-south-asian-film-festi vals-conference [Accessed 2 Aug. 2021].

Vats, V. (2021). Amazon prime rejected The Great Indian Kitchen only to buy it after incredible fan reviews. *IndiaTimes*. [online] Available at: www.indiatimes.com/ entertainment/celebs/amazon-prime-rejected-the-great-indian-kitchen-only-to-buy-it-after-incredible-fan-reviews-537574.html [Accessed 6 Aug. 2021].

6   Essential Indies

Concise case studies

Overview

This chapter comprises condensed appraisals of a selection of seminal independent Indian films spanning the Indie's evolutionary decade from 2010–21. The endeavour is to identify a cross-section of prominent and impactful Indie films that traverse the thematic spectrum mapped out in this book. It is important to reiterate that the selection of films is contingent on discursive, contextual, formal, experimental and receptive singularities that have amplified the presence, visibility and development of new independent Indian films over a decade. These distinctive and diverse facets of new independent Indian cinema contest the restrictive and incorrect categorisation of all Indian films as Bollywood or ersatz regional copies of Bollywood. The concise case studies presented chronologically in this chapter are a hyperlink to the expanded appendix of Indie films presented at the end of this book, with the objective of encouraging engagement with a broader repertoire of influential Indie films spanning a decade of development of this burgeoning sector of Indian cinema.

2010

Peepli Live *(dir. Anusha Rizvi)*

Anusha Rizvi's foundational film set the precedent for a cohesive new wave of independent Indian films to follow. Deploying satirical comedy to represent the exigent theme of a protracted pandemic of farmer suicides in India, the film is an incisive and trenchant critique of political corruption, sensationalist Indian news media, caste-based politics and the inevitable subaltern casualties of these intersecting discourses. The narrative focuses on an impecunious farmer Natha Das Manikpuri (Omkar Das Manikpuri) who is faced with the predicament of losing his land for defaulting on a bank

DOI: 10.4324/9781003089001-7

loan. Natha declares his intention to commit suicide as solitary recourse to gaining government compensation for his beleaguered family. The film bears hallmarks of agrarian-themed postcolonial Indian arthouse films such as *Do Bigha Zamin* (Bimal Roy, 1953) and also draws inspiration from Munshi Premchand's Hindi literary classic *Godaan* (1936) (Archive.indianexpress.com, 2010). *Peepli Live* exemplifies the idiosyncratic and adaptable nature of new independent Indian cinema in terms of casting unknown grassroots folk theatre actor Omkar Das Manikpuri in a central role whilst aligning with mainstream corporate UTV Motion Pictures and Bollywood star-owned Aamir Khan Productions (AKP). The film captures the encounter between rural and urban India through Natha, his poverty-stricken Peepli village and Nandita Malik (Malaika Shenoy), an ambitious and ruthless female TV reporter dispatched by her patriarchal and extractive New Delhi news media channel managers to cover the 'Natha suicide story'. Ultimately, the film's dark comedy premise unveils the nefarious role of Indian politicians striking lucrative deals with multinational conglomerates such as American biotechnology corporation Monsanto whose malfunctioning genetically engineered crop seeds have been cited as a contributing factor to Indian famer suicides. The film serves as a prescient reference point to interpret the actual farmer protests in New Delhi in 2021 against Narendra Modi's plan to corporatise the Indian agricultural sector. The film's discursive and intersectional themes and issues are a blueprint for several subsequent Indian Indies that blend multidimensional formal and stylistic approaches with archetypically Indian topical content.

Dhobi Ghat *(dir. Kiran Rao)*

Alongside *Peepli Live*, this film was another significant release in 2010 marking another female-directed non-Bollywood narrative adopting unconventional stylistic strategies to frame a socio-politically relevant storyline. Kiran Rao's *Dhobi Ghat* (released internationally as *Mumbai Diaries*) harnesses the hyperlink multinarrative film format reminiscent of Hollywood films *Magnolia* (Paul Anderson, 1999) and *Crash* (Paul Haggis, 2004) to map the intersecting lives of four characters in the bustling Indian metropolis of Mumbai. The film is a portrait of class distinctions, economic disparity and marginalised voices that cohabit and collide with more affluent and privileged individuals in the heterotopia of Mumbai. The film's glocal aesthetic and auditory sensibilities are typified by the music score of Oscarwinning Argentinian composer Gustavo Santaolalla which is fused with Indian classical melodies. As a postmodern 'city' film narrated through the hyperlink format with conspicuous interpolation of black and white photographic still frames reminiscent of Sebastião Salgado's snapshots, *Dhobi*

Ghat is one of the pre-eminent forerunners of several subsequent Indie films that would adopt similar hybrid strategies to engage with urban spatiality and socio-economic stratification in modern globalising India.

Harud/Autumn *(dir. Aamir Bashir)*

Aamir Bashir's contemplative Kashmiri-language film was one of the early Indian Indie new wave narratives to confront thematically the suppression of civil liberties by the Indian military presence in the disputed region of Kashmir. Adopting a slow cinema style to mirror the stultifying silence and stasis that pervades the daily lives of ordinary Kashmiri civilians in the tension-filled valley, the film follows in minute detail the aimless perambulations of Rafiq (Shahnawaz Bhat) who is mourning the loss of his missing brother – a photographer arrested and 'disappeared' by Indian security forces. The presence of veteran Iranian actor Reza Naji, who plays Rafiq's father, accentuates comparison of the film's minimalist sensibilities to Iranian arthouse cinema aesthetics. Casting of local non-professional actors, location filming in Kashmir – often under covert and volatile circumstances, a low-budget that was boosted by input from the Hubert Bals Fund and an inevitable censorship struggle with the CBFC over political content demarcate *Harud* as a genuinely Indie film. The film can be framed as an independent counter narrative to reductive, patronising and patriotic Bollywood film representations of Kashmir and its inhabitants. A companion piece to *Harud*, Bashir's *The Winter Within* was in post-production during 2021.

I Am *(dir. Onir)*

Directed by openly gay director Onir, *I Am* is another seminal Indie from the watershed year – 2010. Another example of an Indian Indie adopting the multinarrative hyperlink format, the film is a quartet of stories set across diverse Indian regions, engaging with a corresponding range of pertinent socio-political themes. The first story strand features Afia (Nandita Das), a divorced woman who challenges entrenched social taboos by aiming to bear a child through IVF treatment. The second instalment charts the turbulent homecoming of an exiled Hindu Kashmiri Pandit woman, Megha (Juhi Chawla), estranged from her childhood Muslim friend Rubina (Manisha Koirala) due to the protracted conflict in trouble-torn Kashmir. The third segment is about Abhimanyu (Sanjay Suri), a young man haunted by the recurring spectre of incestuous childhood abuse suffered at the hands of his father. The final story follows the actions of Omar (Arjun Mathur), a young male hustler who seduces Jai (Rahul Bose), a successful gay entrepreneur, and lures him into a compromising situation, whereupon Jai is beaten, sexually assaulted, blackmailed and robbed by a policeman. This graphic portrayal of brutalisation and vilification based on true-life accounts is a metonym for the broader police-inflicted oppression faced by India's LGBTQ+ community. The film was also a timely invocation and interrogation of the infamous anti-gay legislation Section 377 of the Indian Penal Code – a relic of British colonial rule still enforceable at the time of the film's release and only abolished by the Indian Supreme Court in 2018. Notably, *I Am* is the first contemporary Indian film to use crowdfunding, aggregating funds from 400 donors across 45 countries. Following the precedent set by *I Am*, a plethora of Indian Indie filmmakers have adopted crowdfunding as an alternative to mainstream funding sources – particularly films espousing radical, topical or controversial subject matter.

Gandu/Asshole *(dir. Q)*

A controversial film directed by the *enfant terrible* of the new Indian Indie space – Q (Qaushik Mukherjee) who derives inspiration from the subversive and guerrilla filmmaking strategies of Gaspar Noe, Takashi Miike and Khavn De La Cruz. *Gandu* is a nihilistic postmodern rap musical set in Kolkata, charting the directionless and disenfranchised existence of its eponymous socially marginalised teenage character, Gandu, who harbours illusions of becoming a famous rapper and performing alongside the British band Asian Dub Foundation. Gandu meets Ricksha – a slum-dwelling rickshaw puller who becomes Gandu's alter ego, confidant and companion on a psychedelic road trip that sends the characters spiralling into a drug-fuelled abyss. The film's unbridled depictions of full-frontal nudity, graphic sex, drug abuse and explicit dialogue were cited as justification for denial of a certificate of release by the Central Board of Film Certification (CBFC). The film is another Indie exemplar of the concept of the glocal – blending its rap and punk rock music video aesthetic with indigenous Bengali lyrics. Prime-time TV debates around the film's explicit sexual themes, obscenity-ridden screenplay and portrayal of drug dependency set a benchmark in modern Indian cinema in terms of using anarchistic film strategies to tackle traditionally taboo topics.

2011

Dekh Indian Circus/Watch Indian Circus
(dir. Mangesh Hadawale)

Starring two prominent actors from the independent film sector, this film is an allegorical interpretation of rural tribal nomadic communities excluded from India's grand new neoliberal dream. Kajro (Tannishtha Chatterjee) and Jethu (Nawazuddin Siddiqui) face a daily economic struggle to sustain their family in a barren Rajasthan village. The film's central theme involves Kajro's endeavour against all odds to fulfil her children's dream of visiting the travelling 'Great Indian Circus'. Dissecting through its inventive premise and use of comedy the embedded social inequalities, political exploitation and disparity of wealth distribution in contemporary India, this Indie film is a revealing portrait of rural life amongst marginalised social groups.

2012

Ship of Theseus *(dir. Anand Gandhi)*

Anand Gandhi's film has been identified as a philosophical *tour de force* and described by the UK Critics Circle as 'one of 15 global films that can change your life' in a list that includes *Raging Bull, The Battle of Algiers* and *Annie Hall*. The mosaic/hyperlink narrative format is deployed to mirror the film's philosophical premise – Plutarch's Ship of Theseus paradox which questions the authenticity and wholeness of objects that are comprised of multifarious parts. Likewise, the film contains three ostensibly separate story segments that converge at the film's climax. Through its tapestry of western and Indian philosophical concepts, the film is distinctive in its intellectual and introspective ethos, which earmarks it as a watershed moment in the evolution of contemporary Indian cinema. Importantly, through its personification of a young lawyer character, the film discloses the longstanding existence of a nihilistic and atheistic ancient Indian school of thought – *Cārvāka* philosophy which challenged from within the dominant and dogmatic Brahmanical precepts of Hinduism. The film's integration of the hyperlink and anthology story formats is yet another manifestation of Indie films adopting mosaic narratives to tap into India's tug-of-war between the past and present, spirituality and materialism. The film's glocal assemblage is reflected not only through its visual aesthetic, multi-ethnic characters and shifting locales, from Mumbai to Sweden, but also in its multilingual dialogue merging English, Hindi, Marathi, Kannada, Arabic and Swedish. The film's Swedish segment includes striking visual imagery set against the austere rupestrian backdrop of rock formations on Fårö island invoking comparisons with Ingmar Bergman films such as *The Seventh Seal* (1957). Philosophical cross-currents can also be identified in the theme of solitary existential journeys shared between Bergman's *Through a Glass Darkly* (1961), *Wild Strawberries* (1957) and new independent Indian films *Ship of Theseus* and *Dear Molly* (Gajendra Ahire, 2019) (Devasundaram, 2021).

Miss Lovely *(dir. Ashim Ahluwalia)*

The film is an experimental cinematic chronicle of the subterranean C-grade Hindi film industry in Mumbai that straddled a thin line between softcore pornography and low-budget schlock horror in the 1980s and was created to appease a demographic of 'sex-starved' working-class men. In terms of its postmodern formal and stylistic approach, the film calls attention to its own artifice through meta-reference and pastiche of eclectic genre styles such as film noir, verité, crime, romance and melodrama. Director Ashim Ahluwalia describes the C-grade sex-horror films of the 1980s as the 'missing link' between Bollywood and pornography:

> Through these films we can see how Indian society struggles with outlawed subjects: eroticism, violence, female sexuality and homosexuality. If most Bollywood pictures are about the Indian ideal of sameness and the things that bring us together (family, tradition, ritual), C movies are about our differences.
>
> (Ahluwalia, 2014)

The fraternal filmmaking duo in the film, Sonu (Nawazuddin Siddiqui) and Vicky (Anil George), become entangled in a real-world reflection of the seedy, exploitative and sordid diegesis of their own films. Attention to period detail is reflected in the colour palette, production design and costumes of the onscreen characters. The voyeuristic and prurient gaze promoted in the kitschy exploitation films that form the central theme of the film is also mirrored in the production's perspectival, sensorial and stylistic apparatus. *Miss Lovely* epitomises the paradigm shift orchestrated by new independent Indian cinema in terms of hybrid, experimental and syncretic formal approaches delving into marginal facets of Indian culture, society and politics.

Gangs of Wasseypur *(1 and 2) (dir. Anurag Kashyap)*

One of the benchmark films of the Indie new wave directed by Anurag Kashyap, regarded as a pioneer of the independent film movement, this two-part crime thriller is the antithesis of commercial Bollywood with its visceral premise of warring coal mafia family factions in Wasseypur district in the rural hinterlands of Bihar. With its profanity-ridden dialogue, dark humour and graphic violence the film is a postmodern free play on time and space, charting an expanded timeline of politics, local power structures, ethno-religious relations, economic enterprise and cycles of gang violence. The film's hyperlocal credo, explicit style and constellation of actors from the Indie sector are notable features that rendered it an influential and replicable prototype for successful crime-themed Netflix and Amazon Prime Video original web series *Sacred Games* (2018) and *Paatal Lok/Netherworld* (2020).

B.A. Pass *(dir. Ajay Bahl)*

Translocating film noir genre conventions to the neon-lit urban coordinates of backstreet Paharganj in New Delhi, *B.A. Pass* traces the turbulent trajectory of Mukesh (Shadab Kamal), an orphaned teenager who migrates from a small town to the big city. Unable to fund his undergraduate studies and support his sisters, Mukesh becomes a male gigolo at the disposal of affluent housewives in New Delhi. On the surface, the film appears to be a conventional plot-twisting erotic neo-noir thriller. On a subtextual level, the narrative focalises the predicament of the subaltern, in this case the exploitation of a rural migrant in the unremitting urban space. Socio-economic and class disparities are assessed in the film which contrasts the upper-class privilege of the sybaritic housewives with the abjection of the young teenager and his vulnerable sisters. At titular and thematic levels, the film highlights the denial of education to India's underprivileged underclass who are compelled to eke out a living by any means possible. The film therefore reflects the protean engagement of Indie films with a multiplicity of formal and stylistic templates in the telling of unconventional storylines, often from the perspectives of powerless and marginalised subaltern characters.

2013

Lucia *(dir. Pawan Kumar)*

Karnataka-based director Pawan Kumar's Kannada film is distinctive for its inventive social media and internet-based crowdfunding strategy. Kumar accumulated the equivalent of £51,000 from crowdfunding via an intensive awareness and publicity campaign conducted through Facebook and other digital platforms. Gaining his target budget in 27 days, Kumar refers to his methodology as 'instant cinema'. Kumar also established his own video-on-demand online portal Home Talkies, offering his films to subscribers for a fee. *Lucia* traces the journey of Nikki (Satish Ninasam), a small town migrant worker in Bangalore, Karnataka's capital city often referred to as the 'Silicon Valley of India'. Working unconventional hours as an usher in a fleapit cinema and beset by insomnia, Nikki is offered a sleeping pill by a louche drug dealer. He finds himself plunged into a surreal sensorium of lucid dreams where he lives out his fantasies of becoming a film megastar.

Playing with space and time and utilising fluid cinematography to break the fourth wall, *Lucia* is significantly different from the traditional conventions of regional Kannada cinema. As an independent film from South India, the film was markedly impactful at the box-office and was screened at multiplexes across the country. *Lucia* also won the Audience Choice Award at the London Indian Film Festival (LIFF) in 2013. Kumar was able to sell the film's Hindi, Tamil and Telugu remake rights to major production houses such as Fox Star.

Papilio Buddha *(dir. Jayan Cherian)*

Kerala filmmaker Jayan Cherian's controversial film is a trenchant dissection of routinised caste-discrimination faced by rural 'lower-caste' Dalit and tribal Adivasi communities who face eviction from their land by government and police forces. Involving the participation of Dalit communities and Dalit Human Rights Movement (DHRM) activists, the film adopts a minimalist and realist aesthetic palette to narrate the local grassroots struggle of subaltern Dalits who have historically been persecuted by the retrenched caste system in Hinduism. The caste hierarchy relegates them to sub-human status and performers of menial tasks such as scavenging, cremating dead bodies and removing refuse. Several Indies spanning 2010 to 2021 have challenged the status quo of 'upper-caste' privilege that places Brahmin Hindus at the apex of the caste pyramid. *Papilio Buddha* stands out for its visceral portrayal of violence on Dalits, the routinised sexual violation faced by Dalit women and the ecological destruction wreaked by state-sanctioned corporations. Through strategic lighting, a muted colour palette and the pregnant pauses of slow cinema the film evokes an oneiric sensorial stasis that mirrors the imposed inertia on the oppressed Dalit community who exist in perpetual fear of being displaced from their land. Denied a certificate of release in India allegedly for denigrating national icons such as Mahatma Gandhi and for portraying homosexuality, the film was disqualified from screening at the International Film Festival of Kerala (IFFK). An alternative private screening was disrupted by police intervention, epitomising the stifling of dissenting narratives in contemporary India.

The Lunchbox *(dir. Ritesh Batra)*

A globally acclaimed and commercially successful Indian Indie, *The Lunchbox* is significant as a transnational co-production. Developed by the NFDC Screenwriters Lab initiative, *The Lunchbox* is an archetypical example of a glocal Indian Indie. The film's universal aesthetic sensibilities are blended with its locally situated but broadly relatable storyline. An aging middle-class clerk Sajan Fernandes (Irrfan Khan) on the verge of retirement from his bureaucratic office job becomes engaged in an unlikely epistolary romance with a young housewife, Ila (Nimrat Kaur), trapped in a loveless marriage. Akin to its 'city' film predecessor *Dhobi Ghat* also set in Mumbai, *The Lunchbox* draws attention to moribund cultural spaces such as the iconic Irani cafes which were established by the dwindling Parsi community – descendants of Zoroastrian Persian migrants who settled in India in the 9th century. Delving into deeper themes of nostalgia, memory and displacement, *The Lunchbox* contains layered discourses linking to India's socialist past and its indiscriminate urbanisation typifying the nation's neoliberal future. Ritesh Batra went on to echo this nostalgia for the socialist days of 1980s India in *Photograph* (2018) – another film set in Mumbai featuring ordinary individuals brought together across the class and religious divide.

Fandry/Pig *(dir. Nagraj Manjule)*

Dalit filmmaker Nagraj Manjule's pathbreaking Marathi drama film is a coming of age story of a 'lower-caste' boy, Jabya (Somnath Awghade), who dares to challenge the impermeable caste divide when he seeks the amorous attention of Shalu (Rajeshwari Kharat) – an 'upper-caste' girl. Manjule has achieved significant commercial and critical success with his debut film *Fandry* and his sophomore project *Sairat/Wild* (2016), both of which foreground and bring to the mainstream issues of caste discrimination in contemporary India. Independent films that centralise Dalit themes are all the more important considering commercial Bollywood films have largely disavowed or erased Dalit identity and excluded representation of Dalit lived experience.

2014

Court *(dir. Chaitanya Tamhane)*

Chaitanya Tamhane's film is conspicuous for the plethora of international film festival plaudits exceeding 24 awards worldwide. Exemplifying the independent filmmaking sector's engagement with the prominent Indian issue of caste-based oppression, *Court* harnesses an aesthetic of verisimilitude and local realism to chart the arrest of an elderly Dalit folk singer and civil rights crusader Narayan Kamble (played by true-life activist the late Vira Sathidar, himself a victim of police surveillance and oppression) on the fabricated charge of singing seditionary political folk songs that spurred a man to commit suicide. The protracted and farcical courtroom trial that follows is Kafkaesque and reflects the institutional bureaucracy, corruption and reactionary religious ideology that underpin legal structures and social mentalities in modern India. The film's narrative presents a polarised vision of neoliberal India by foregrounding the religious superstitions of the presiding court judge and the xenophobic Hindu nationalist sensibility of the prosecuting lawyer alongside the liberal bourgeois mindset of the barrister representing the Dalit defendant. Through its minimalist aesthetic and measured pacing the film seems to anticipate the true-life arrest and arbitrary incarceration of 16 pro-Dalit human rights activists on falsified charges by the Indian state in the 2018 Bhima Koregaon case.

Unfreedom *(dir. Raj Amit Kumar)*

Deemed controversial owing to its portrayal of a lesbian romance and religious fundamentalism, this is another example of an Indie film denied a certificate of release by the CBFC. The filmmaker raised an appeal at the High Court which was denied and the enjoinment on the film upheld. Adopting the catchphrase 'banned in India' as a selling point akin to Q's proscribed film *Gandu*, Raj Amit Kumar relied on the international film festival circuit as a mechanism of proliferation. Featuring renowned actors such as Victor Banerjee and Adil Hussain, the film is a scathing interrogation of police brutalisation of the LGBTQ+ community. The Indian police station as a space of exception where the rule of law can be suspended arbitrarily (Devasundaram, 2018) is visualised with graphic and visceral detail in the film.

Margarita With a Straw *(dir. Shonali Bose)*

The film is based on the director's cousin Malini Chib's memoir *One Little Finger* (2010) documenting her experience of living with cerebral palsy. Broaching twin themes of disability and lesbian identity through the perspective of a young woman, Laila (Kalki Koechlin), *Margarita With a Straw* is a glocal film presenting a globally relatable visual aesthetic as the capsule for the story of Laila's journey into finding love, exploring sexuality and discovering self-acceptance. The appearance in the film of English actor William Moseley, recognisable from *The Chronicles of Narnia* (2005), and locales straddling Delhi and New York demonstrates the film's hybrid sensibilities. Centralising the perspectives and sexuality of a differently-abled protagonist – themes often overlooked or essentialised in mainstream Indian cinema, the transcontinental journal of self-discovery undertaken by Laila is a candid evaluation of alterity, belonging and identity. In this regard, Amy Villarejo's (2018) essay on 'queer radiance' is a probing study of the film's intersectional themes of gender, sexuality and disability.

Killa/the fort *(dir. Avinash Arun)*

Typifying the multidimensionality of the Indies, this Marathi film produced and distributed by indigenous Indie-focused JAR Pictures utilises the family drama format to narrate its coming-of-age story as experienced by its central character, a fatherless 11-year-old boy in a picturesque Konkan coast village. When the boy befriends a band of local village boys, they embark on a bicycle adventure of exploration that leads them to discover a mysterious fort. Evocative cinematography by director Avinash Arun capturing the scenic local environment alongside underplayed central performances exemplify the independent attributes of the film which won the Crystal Bear award at the Berlin Film Festival. Director Avinash Arun has subsequently gone on to co-direct Amazon Prime Video series *Paatal Lok* (2020).

Haider *(dir. Vishal Bhardwaj)*

Vishal Bhardwaj's indigenised adaptation of Shakespeare's *Hamlet* is translocated to the conflict zone of Kashmir. Bollywood star Shahid Kapoor plays Haider – an angst-ridden young man haunted by the spectre of his absent father who has been abducted by the Indian army. The film undertakes an unflinching and incisive reinterpretation of regional politics through its trenchant critique of the Armed Forces Special Powers Act (AFSPA) which grants Indian military forces carte blanche powers to use lethal force with impunity including licence to enter Kashmiri civilian homes and arrest anyone suspected of insurgency. These arbitrary powers have led to the disappearance of thousands of young and old Kashmiri men, whisked away from their homes and families by the Indian army, never to be seen again. The film reveals that a derelict cinema hall has been repurposed into a detention and torture centre for disappeared Kashmiri men by the Indian army. *Haider* displays a hybrid blend of Indie and Bollywood characteristics in the realm of its casting choices, melodrama, music and action sequences. However, the film's unequivocal and trenchant political content epitomises the facet that distinguishes new wave Indie films from their commercial Bollywood counterparts.

2015

Angry Indian Goddesses *(dir. Pan Nalin)*

Promoted as India's first all-female buddy road film, genre conventions are deployed to foreground a modern feminist perspective focalised on seven Indian women of diverse persuasions. Featuring an ensemble cast of Indie actors ranging from Sandhya Mridul and Tannishtha Chatterjee to Adil Hussain, the film illustrates the ironic paradigm of venerated and deified Hindu goddesses in Indian society contrasted by sexual violence, rape and abuse suffered routinely by women in everyday life. The film's prismatic portrayal of the seven female friends who congregate for a weekend in Goa facilitates a subjective insight into a cross-section of urban Indian female identities. The resident housemaid's local working-class background – in stark contrast with the more affluent class ante-cedents of the friend circle – does not form a barrier to establishment of female solidarities in the film. The persistent psychological fear of rape and sexual abuse amongst women in India is reified in the film when a tragic event shatters the group's idyllic sojourn. Concomitant with its nuanced and uninhibited treatment of same-sex marriage, the denouement of *Angry Indian Goddesses* is an intensive filmic articula-tion of resistance to misogynistic, bigoted and homophobic institutions and attitudes in contemporary India.

Masaan *(dir. Neeraj Ghaywan)*

Exemplifying the popularity of the hyperlink, multi-strand narrative for-mat, *Masaan* utilises as its canvas the ancient Hindu holy town of Varanasi for its intersecting storylines. The film's iconography of the Ganges flow-ing past the sacred Hindu cremation *ghats* smouldering along the riverbank is a symbolic representation of impermanence and liminality. In this con-text, *Masaan* is a tapestry of the confluence between tradition and tech-nology, illustrating India's seesawing between the past and present. With its intersectional themes relating to gender-based discrimination, patriar-chy, caste-prejudice and police corruption, the film is a striking example of unconventional form, style and content characteristic of Indie films and divergent from Bollywood.

Parched *(dir. Leena Yadav)*

This is a prominent example of a bona fide F-Rated female-centric film, writ-ten and directed by Leena Yadav and focusing on the lives of four women in a barren hinterland of Gujarat. Cinematography by Russell Carpenter and editing by Kevin Tent exemplify the glocal facets of this film production. *Parched* follows the individual struggles of the quartet of women against a brutally oppressive patriarchy that undergirds the constellation of rural life, from the village elders' absolute governing authority to routinised misogy-nistic social structures. The embodiment of female resistance emerges in the form of Bijli (Surveen Chawla) – a demimonde dancer who makes a living as a travelling circus tent performer of sexually explicit Bollywood 'item number' songs for the baying gratification and prurient appeasement of the village men. The elemental difference in the film's adoption of the Bollywood-style item number is the self-critical subversion of the formulaic Bollywood song and dance set-piece largely celebrated in Indian culture. By contextualising the item number as pernicious and dehumanising to women, the film mounts a narrative of resistance to Bollywood's popular imagination of women as sex objects.

Island City *(dir. Ruchika Oberoi)*

This is a triple narrative portmanteau film featuring story segments that engage with the vicissitudes and contradictions of contemporary neoliberal India. The first story deals with the soul-destroying functionality of a corporate office and its jaded employees. The second storyline features a repressed housewife, her young son and her elderly mother browbeaten on a daily basis by the wife's authoritarian and misogynistic husband. The third instalment follows the female perspective of a dutiful daughter in a working-class household who is coerced by her parents into accepting the courtship and marriage proposal of a louche and sexist man. *Island City* is similar to other Indies such as *Dhobi Ghat, Ship of Theseus* and *Photograph* in its use of the 'city film' strategy, portraying intersecting human narratives within the urban space of Mumbai. This film is distinctive in its discursive and spatial engagement with the domestic, corporate and sociocultural milieu in contemporary India through the perspectives of ordinary individuals, particularly women.

Visaranai *(dir. Vertrimaaran)*

This independent Tamil film is based on the true-life experience of Dalit author and autorickshaw driver M. Chandrakumar as documented in his book *Lock-Up: Jottings of an Ordinary Man* (2017). Four 'lower-caste' Dalit Tamil migrant workers in neighbouring Andhra Pradesh state are arrested on a false charge, incarcerated and tortured in a local police station. Exposing the interconnections between political power and law enforcement, *Visaranai* is a visceral rendition of caste-based discrimination and police brutalisation of minority and marginalised communities in India. *Visaranai* is also uncannily clairvoyant in its foreshadowing of the particularly gruesome police-inflicted custodial torture and murder in Tamil Nadu of father and son P. Jayaraj and J. Bennicks who were arrested allegedly for keeping their shop open beyond authorised hours during the Covid-19 lockdown in 2020. The film is a visceral exposé of entitlement, impunity and absolute power wielded disproportionately by the Indian police against religious, ethnic, caste and sexual minorities.

Thithi *(dir. Raam Reddy)*

This is an example of a low-budget hyperlocal independent Kannada-language Indian film with spartan production values that attained global recognition. Notably, the film features an entire cast of village residents from the agrarian region of Mandya district in southern Karnataka state. Adopting black comedy satire as its medium, the film's centrepiece is the titular *thithi* – a post-funeral commemorative ceremony, held to mark the 11th day since the death of local centenarian 'Century' Gowda (Singri Gowda). An intergenerational feud ensues amongst the old patriarch's descendants who manoeuvre to inherit his land. Gaining accolades including the Golden Leopard award at the Locarno International Film Festival and a National Film Award, Raam Reddy's debut feature is an Indo-American co-production, epitomising the Indies' ability to narrate locally specific Indian-themed content through globally relatable storytelling often utilising the conduit of international film co-production.

Loev *(dir. Sudhanshu Saria)*

Presenting a positive and optimistic portrayal of LGBTQ+ identity in modern India, *Loev* (an intentional malapropism of 'love') focuses on young gay male Indian lived experiences in an urban setting. Adopting road film genre conventions, the film navigates the weekend getaway of Sahil (Dhruv Ganesh) and his childhood friend Jai (Shiv Pandit), as they rekindle the flame of a lingering but unfulfilled romance. Repressed and open homosexual identities in a heteronormative cultural milieu is one of the key themes in the film. Sudhanshu Saria takes a detour from conventionally tragic renditions of gay-themed stories which either manifest in the brutalisation, victimisation or murder of homosexual characters. The hopeful and naturalistic portrayal of everyday vicissitudes in the lives of young gay men in Mumbai sets a benchmark in terms of normalising LGBTQ+ identities in contemporary Indian cinema.

2016

Aligarh *(dir. Hansal Mehta)*

Hansal Mehta's pathbreaking film, written and edited by gay Indian editor/screenwriter Apurva Asrani, was released at a pivotal moment in the campaign to abolish the archaic British colonial-era anti-homosexuality legislation Section 377. Playing an important role in foregrounding the need for openness, tolerance and acceptance towards LGBTQ+ identity, the film's promotional #ComeOutandQuestion catchphrase is reflected in its portrayal of true-life incidents where elderly professor Ramchandra Siras at Aligarh Muslim University became the victim of a tabloid media sting operation. A local TV film crew invaded his home and filmed him having sex with a Muslim rickshaw puller, leading to his sacking and eviction from staff lodging by the university. Highlighting the complicity of the university authorities in the media operation, the film is a contemplative evaluation of regressive institutional and social attitudes towards Siras's homosexuality and the loneliness and isolation of his daily life. Notably, the film also dissects the universalised western nomenclatural category 'gay' appraising its hermetic limitations when applied to nuanced contexts that expose the arbitrary and performative actuality of sexuality and gender categories. Prof. Siras (Manoj Bajpayee) in the film considers the term 'gay' a problematic encapsulation – inadequate in capturing a range of emotions and ineffable sentiments in its 'three letters'.

Lipstick Under My Burkha *(dir. Alankrita Shrivastava)*

Presenting a ground-breaking and polarising feminist perspective, *Lipstick Under My Burkha* was deemed controversial and in the words of the erstwhile Chairman of the CBFC Pahlaj Nihalani too 'lady oriented' to be given a certificate of release. Set in small town Bhopal, the film follows the lives of four age-diverse women. Reactionary and misogynistic attitudes thwart their aspirations, agency and sexuality. Following global media exposure and accolades received across a plethora of international film festivals, the film was eventually allowed to be screened in India after prescribed cuts were implemented. *Lipstick Under My Burkha* galvanised animated community conversations amongst the South Asian diaspora when it was screened at Leicester, Edinburgh and London editions of the UK Asian Film Festival (UKAFF) in 2017. With its distinctly feminist ethos, this is another example of an F-Rated film, written and directed by Alankrita Shrivastava and starring four prominent female actors. Shrivastava's subsequent work includes the female-themed *Dolly Kitty and Those Twinkling Stars* (2019) and the Netflix series *Bombay Begums* (2021).

A Death in the Gunj *(dir. Konkona Sen Sharma)*

Prolific Indian Indie actor Konkona Sen Sharma's directorial debut is a nostalgic and oneiric family drama mystery set during 1979 in the erstwhile

Anglo-Indian heritage town of McCluskieganj in Jharkhand state. The narrative is oriented around gauche and introverted university student Shutu (Vikrant Massey) whose reunion with family and friends in a colonial-era bungalow spirals into a sinuous shadow play of sexual desire, hypermasculinity, repressed passions, secrets and vendettas. Divergent from Bollywood in its aesthetic style, unconventional theme and English dialogue *A Death in the Gunj* exhibits meticulous mise-en-scene and attention to period detail. It also features an ensemble cast of Indie actors including Kalki Koechlin, Gulshan Deviah, Tillotama Shome and Ranvir Shorey.

Sairat/Wild *(dir. Nagraj Manjule)*

This low-budget Marathi independent film's focal point is a doomed romance between young lovers who defy the caste barrier. Self-produced and co-written by Dalit director Nagraj Manjule, the film was a resounding critical and commercial success spawning several regional language remakes in India. With its hybrid approach, utilising song sequences, vibrant colour design and romance genre conventions, the film is an accessible and pluralistic capsule to highlight the violent ramifications of inter-caste intimacy and marriage in India. The film therefore is a masterful strategy to challenge the seemingly impregnable caste status quo. *Sairat* also draws attention to the prevailing political dispensation of the BJP whose rule has witnessed normalisation of brutal and murderous attacks on young couples who disregard Hindu fundamentalist rules forbidding miscegenation not only between 'upper' and 'lower' caste lovers but also interfaith marriages between Hindu and Muslim couples.

2017

Mukti Bhawan/Hotel Salvation *(dir. Shubhashish Bhutiani)*

Similar to *Masaan*, the film harnesses the evocative location of Varanasi, the ancient Hindu holy town on the banks of the river Ganges. The town's significance to Hindus as a cremation site from where it is believed human souls ascend directly to heaven has correlation to the film's title. The eponymous Mukti Bhawan/Hotel Salvation is a halfway home for elderly retirees who wish to spend their last days in contemplation and serenity. A senior patriarch Daya (Lalit Behl) who lives with his marketing professional son Rajiv's (Adil Hussain) family in Mumbai has a moment of epiphany where he decides to expend his twilight days in the Hotel Salvation. Overriding the inevitable opposition from his son, daughter-in-law and granddaughter, Daya ensconces himself in the spartan surroundings of the salvific sanctuary of his desire. The film's philosophical tone is infused with existential themes, ideas of reincarnation, afterlife and family bonds. With its Varanasi setting, the film is distinctive in its decoupling from the ubiquitous urban setting of big city films. The visual imagery and mood evoked by the film fold into subtle and overt gallows humour as a strategy to confront mortality and separation. The schisms between father and son present a naturalistic perspective of intergenerational difference which is a noteworthy divergence from the predictable filial piety stereotypical of Bollywood films. *Mukti Bhawan*/*Hotel Salvation* was Shubhashish Bhutiani's debut feature film and he was 26-years old at the time of its release, underscoring the Indies as a domain for burgeoning filmmaking talent. The glocal appeal of this Indie film is reflected in its acquisition, promotion and release in the UK by the British Film Institute (BFI).

2018

Soni *(dir. Ivan Ayr)*

This independent Indian film centres on the eponymous female police officer, as she navigates the bureaucratic and male-dominated arena of the Delhi police force. Adopting a realist aesthetic, muted colour scheme, tenebrous lighting and tight camera framing, the film presents an insight into impenetrable hierarchies, a misogynistic chain of command, political intervention and the female solidarity between Soni and her senior superintendent colleague. This *esprit de corps* becomes indispensable as the two women battle gender-based violence on Delhi streets and navigate the conventionalised police force patriarchy that hampers their autonomy and career prospects.

Hamid *(dir. Aijaz Khan)*

Hamid is a potent visual chronicle of the dehumanising effects of conflict on both sides of the battleline in the trouble-torn region of Kashmir. The film's singular premise imagines an unlikely friendship forged over a mobile phone between the titular 8-year-old Kashmiri boy whose father has been forcibly disappeared by occupying Indian military forces, and an Indian army soldier suffering from combat shock. Akin to its Indie counterparts *Harud*, *Side A and Side B* and *No Fathers in Kashmir*, *Hamid* presents a grassroots perspective of the disruptive impact stemming from Indian military occupation in Kashmir and the innumerable ghosts of vanished Kashmiri civilian fathers, sons and brothers in the valley. However, *Hamid* stands apart in its understated and negotiatory tone – a reflective child's-eye-view of a complex situation illustrating the futility of violent conflict. Local Kashmiri Talha Arshad Reshi, in his first film role, won the National Film Award for Best Child Artist in 2019. The pristine aesthetic backdrop of the Himalayan landscape is harnessed through the film's cinematography to connect local Kashmiris and their land, reiterating the Indian Indies' use of local realism to capture everyday lived experiences of oppressed and marginalised individuals and communities. Screened at the UK Asian Film Festival (UKAFF), *Hamid* eventually found a platform on Netflix.

Evening Shadows *(dir. Sridhar Rangayan)*

Sridhar Rangayan has been at the vanguard of LGBTQ+ activism through the aegis of his independent production company Solaris pictures which has focused exclusively on a diverse spectrum of LGBTQIA+ themes. His film *Evening Shadows*, draws on the local aesthetics of a small town in Rangayan's native state of Karnataka in South India to challenge retrenched heteronormative, homophobic and orthodox religious attitudes towards sexual orientation and identity in traditional Indian domestic structures. The film charts the homecoming of Kartik (Devansh Doshi), a young gay man who keeps his sexuality hidden from his traditional Brahmin Hindu mother, Vasudha (Mona Ambegaonkar), and father, Damodar (Ananth Mahadevan). The film's narrative is positioned strategically in terms of its temporal setting on the cusp of the Indian Supreme Court's verdict in 2013 upholding the antiquated British colonial-era anti-homosexuality legislation – Section 377. As the film's postscript reveals prior to the end credits, Section 377 was later abolished in a landmark ruling by the Supreme Court in 2018. Similar to several other independent Indian productions, *Evening Shadows* is a low-budget film created through a combination of crowdfunding, self-investment and private investor contributions. The film has since gained global visibility through screenings at the UK Asian Film Festival – UKAFF 2019 and accessibility on Netflix.

2019

No Fathers in Kashmir *(dir. Ashvin Kumar)*

Oscar-nominated documentarian Ashvin Kumar applies a minimalist aesthetic and the coming-of-age idiom to this narrative feature interpretation of human rights violations by Indian armed forces in disputed Kashmir. Adopting a characteristic Indie glocal approach, the film charts the relationship between British-Kashmiri teenager Noor (Zara Webb) on a homecoming visit and local Kashmiri adolescent Majid (Shivam Raina). As signified by the film's title, both teenagers' fathers, themselves friends, were forcibly 'disappeared' by the occupying Indian army. The film's critical premise embroiled Ashvin Kumar in a protracted censorship struggle with the CBFC which prescribed several cuts to the film. After petitioning the now defunct Film Certification Appellate Tribunal (FCAT) repeatedly and following a compromise in the form of cuts and disclaimers, Kumar's film finally gained a release in 2019. Embodying the independent Indian film sector's critical and political appraisals of the controversial Kashmir issue which are antithetical to Bollywood's biased and nationalistic renditions, *No Fathers in Kashmir* typifies the predicament of Indie films with polemical political content that immediately invoke repressive measures by the state's regulatory apparatus.

Article 15 *(dir. Anubhav Sinha)*

A hybrid film that typifies the idiosyncratic faculty of new Indian Indie films to juxtapose casting of prominent Bollywood stars with sociopolitically incisive thematic content. In this film, mainstream actor Ayushmann Khurrana essays the role of an idealistic Indian Police Service (IPS) officer who is dispatched to a remote rural village to investigate the gruesome rape, murder and tree-hanging of two Dalit women. Reminiscent of the visual aesthetic and theme of murdered civil rights workers and racial violence in Alan Parker's *Mississippi Burning* (1988), *Article 15* opens a similar investigative 'can of worms', specifically from the Indian context of caste discrimination. Blending police procedural, thriller and drama genres the film investigates entrenched structural and social caste bias that intersects with misogyny and crystallises in sexual violence, rape and murder. The eponymous Article 15 refers to the 15th article of the Indian constitution which prohibits discrimination on the basis of religion, caste, sex or place of birth. The film's premise is a fictionalised interpretation of true events surrounding the 2014 gangrape and murder of two teenage women in Badaun district of Uttar Pradesh and is a notable example of an Indie centralising the sensitive issue of caste-based gender violence.

Kattumaram/Catamaran *(dir. Swarnavel Eswaran)*

Distinctive in its portrayal of female same-sex desire in a remote coastal fishing village in Tamil Nadu, the film's picturesque rural aesthetics form the backdrop for its navigation of cross-class lesbian love between an indigent local fisherman's niece and a visiting schoolteacher from the city. Patriarchal familial structures, homophobic attitudes and economic privation are intersecting themes in this evocative interpretation of women from polarised backgrounds finding love in the rural space. The film screened at several festivals including the Frameline: San Francisco International LGBT Film Festival, Kashish Mumbai International Queer Film Festival and London Indian Film Festival in 2019.

Photograph *(dir. Ritesh Batra)*

A companion piece to *The Lunchbox*, Ritesh Batra's film picks up the thread of representing ordinary people finding love across India's class and religious borders. A working-class Muslim street photographer (Nawazuddin Siddiqui) captures an image of a shy and introverted young woman (Sanya Malhotra) from a conservative middle-class Hindu background against the iconic backdrop of Mumbai's Gateway of India. This visual document, analogous to the lunchbox in Batra's previous film, serves as a connecting link that brings the unconventional couple together. The visual canvas of Mumbai is once again adopted as a local landscape that plays a pivotal role in the couple's interactions but also as a hyperlink to assessing India's socialist past in the 1980s, returning to themes of nostalgia, urban transformation and national memory broached by *The Lunchbox*.

Raahgir/The Wayfarers *(dir. Goutam Ghose)*

Reincarnating the arthouse aesthetic of Satyajit Ray, *Raahgir/The Wayfarers* is directed by eminent filmmaker Goutam Ghose who is a self-professed votary of Ray. The film centralises a strong female role by well-known actor Tillotama Shome alongside her compatriots from the Indie sector Adil Hussain, Omkar Das Manikpuri and Neeraj Kabi. Set in the tribal heartland of Jharkhand, the narrative follows the adventitious convergence of two itinerant strangers – Nathuni (Shome) and Lakhua (Hussain) – both seeking daily wage work. Along the road, the two travellers respond altruistically to a beleaguered man (Kabi) who implores them to help him dislodge his motor vehicle stuck in a quagmire. The collective solidarity displayed by the motley crew of three strangers who push the outlandish vehicle all the way to the motorway is a metaphor for India's erstwhile socialist 'unity in diversity' ideal, communitarian spirit and secular constitutional ethos eroded since the 1990s by liberalisation and the rise of Hindutva politics. The film's unadorned aesthetics speak to the social realism of Satyajit Ray and other postcolonial Indian filmmakers such as Bimal Roy, Mrinal Sen and Ritwik Ghatak. Apart from socio-political themes, *Raahgir* harnesses the road film trope of transformational journeys undertaken by picaresque and subaltern characters, emphasising the Indian Indie aspects of this film.

2020

Axone *(dir. Nicholas Kharkongor)*

Exemplifying an increasing number of independent films emerging from India's North Eastern states, *Axone* traces the daily lived experience of a group of young Nagaland migrants in New Delhi. North Eastern individuals often face regularised xenophobic prejudice and violence in Delhi and the rest of 'mainland' India. Disconcerting dimensions of socio-economic exclusion and bigotry along ethnic lines are couched in comedy in *Axone*. The Naga friends are lodgers in the house of an authoritarian Delhi landlady who monitors their every move and appraises every visitor to the household. The friends wish to hold a clandestine wedding reception in their spartan rented rooms by cooking an esoteric fermented soyabean dish – axone (pronounced 'akhuni') – a notoriously malodorous yet delicious Naga culinary delicacy. The film's appraisal of food-based ethno-religious discrimination is particularly relevant in contemporary India, where the BJP government's ban on beef consumption is coterminous with a spate of Hindu nationalist 'cow vigilante' murders of Muslim dairy farmers.

Kalla Nottam/*The False Eye (dir. Rahul Riji Nair)*

Exemplifying the experimentation with form and style that distinguishes the new Indies from Bollywood, the entire narrative of this Malayalam film by Kerala-based director Rahul Riji Nair is captured from the visual perspective of a GoPro camera which starts its life cycle as a surveillance camera in a local grocery shop. This all-seeing-eye is stolen by two young boys who dream of making their own film with the gadget. Invariably, the camera captures an expansive collage of the local landscape and everyday interactions as it changes hands. Utilising the subjective panopticon perspective of the GoPro lens, the film bears witness to topical themes and issues at local level that are relatable to generalised and systematised practices in India. Misogyny and voyeuristic vigilante moral policing are at the forefront of the film's socio-political agenda. Accused of thieving by a couple of adult men, the young boys who pilfered the camera become embroiled in the men's attempt to adopt the camera as a spying and documenting device to publicly shame a young couple engaging in a surreptitious intimate moment in a secluded grove. The theme of vigilante moral policing enforced arbitrarily on couples displaying affection in public and private spaces is an echo of previous Indies such as *Love, Sex Aur Dhokha (LSD)*, *Aligarh* and *Masaan*. The film's premise has a factual basis in regular incidents of violent curtailment and socio-religious control of sexual expression in India.

Kalla Nottam is distinctive in its inventive formal and stylistic approach to exposing repressive patriarchy and gender bias in interior domestic and exterior public spheres in India.

Serious Men *(dir. Sudhir Mishra)*

Applying the satirical comedy treatment to topical themes and issues, *Serious Men* is similar to other Indies such as *Peepli Live* and *Newton* that draw on ironic humour to confront systemic injustices and socio-economic disparities in modern India. The film focuses on entrenched caste prejudice and watertight class structures through the eyes of a 'lower-caste' young boy who is publicised as a child savant through a subterfuge devised by his overambitious father Ayyan Mani (Nawazuddin Siddiqui). Tenement-dwelling Mani holds a subordinate position at an elite national research institute in Mumbai, where he is continually debased and humiliated by the supercilious Brahmin director of research. Aspirational and irrepressible in his desire for social mobility, Mani's elaborate contrivance to promote his little son as an omniscient mathematics genius involves the boy wearing a covert earpiece whilst his father stationed remotely supplies the boy with answers to live audience questions. When the deception is uncovered, the layers of caste and class domination are unpacked and shortcomings of the rote-based Indian primary education system laid bare for scrutiny by the film. This singular satirical filmic treatment of serious themes underscores the diverse spectrum of approaches undertaken by Indies to espouse heterodox content.

2021

The Great Indian Kitchen *(dir. Jeo Baby)*

This pathbreaking Malayalam film set in the southern Indian state of Kerala maps the coeval prevalence of patriarchal power and religious orthodoxy inside and outside traditional Indian family structures. Narrated from the perspective of a young newlywed housewife, the film's ironic title demarcates the kitchen as the site where culinary customs are churned together with gendered roles and the subordination of women to domesticity. The film documents the repetitive mundane daily household chores of the wife (Nimisha Sajayan) in her conservative in-laws' traditional home where she is effectively incarcerated in the kitchen. This film is a melting pot of micro and macro level political discourses relating to patriarchy focusing specifically on the Indian Supreme Court ruling that overturned an anachronistic Hindu precept forbidding women of menstruating age entry into Kerala's sacred Sabarimala temple which is a pilgrimage site for male Hindu devotees. This national level debate is mediated within the domestic interiority of the Wife's home, where she is quarantined in her room and deemed 'untouchable' whilst she has her menstrual period. Faced with relentless debasement and segregation, the Wife decides to break the patriarchal and ritualistic shackles by sharing a Facebook post from a feminist activist exhorting Indian women to hail the Supreme Court verdict as a general call for female emancipation. Gaining global attention for its radical and iconoclastic female-led narrative, *The Great Indian Kitchen* screened at the UK Asian Film Festival 2021 and was acquired eventually by Amazon Prime Video.

Toofan Mail *(dir. Akriti Singh)*

Fulfilling the triune criteria of the F-Rating yardstick, *Toofan Mail* is the directorial debut of Akriti Singh who also wrote and starred in the film. Drawing on formal and aesthetic sensibilities reminiscent of Parallel film auteur Mani Kaul and postcolonial arthouse cinema doyen Satyajit Ray, *Toofan Mail* is an interpretation of a historical incident in 1974 involving a woman professing to be the Queen of Awadh who deposits herself and her entourage in a railway station in New Delhi demanding to hold court with the then Indian Prime Minister Indira Gandhi. The film's idiosyncratic premise and its whimsical, oneiric aura is an inventive capsule to illustrate how rupturing moments in Indian history such as the first war of Indian independence in 1857 and the imposition of a state of Emergency in the 1970s were prefigurative symptoms of broader political and social instability. This provides the contextual basis for the film's implicit signposting of draconian measures by Narendra Modi's BJP government to curb freedom and civil liberties, reflective of a general state of repressive authoritarianism in modern India.

Sherni *(dir. Amit Masurkar)*

Starring Bollywood actor Vidya Balan and distributed on Amazon Prime Video, this film exhibits quintessentially Indie attributes in its stylistic and thematic construction. Balan plays Vidya Vincent, a tenacious and idealistic female officer in the Indian Forest Service (IFS) stationed in a remote jungle outpost to solve the quandary of a man-eating tigress whose close proximity to impoverished cattle herder villagers has exacerbated the conflict between natural environment and human survival. The film's naturalistic style synchronises with its ecological theme which in turn intersects with the barrier of institutional patriarchy, political nepotism and corruption that pervades the IFS hierarchy, thwarting the figurative *sherni* (tigress) Vincent's endeavours to safeguard the forest's threatened tigers and the tribal villagers. Ultimately, Vincent is demoted and reassigned to a functionary position in another location, demonstrating the hegemonic power of a patriarchal state.

References

Ahluwalia, A. (2014). Ashim Ahluwalia | Radical raunch. *mint*. [online] Available at: www.livemint.com/Leisure/59ZqEmAt8jKBPupwwWeaVP/Ashim-Ahlu walia – Radical-raunch.html [Accessed 6 Apr. 2016].

Archive.indianexpress.com. (2010). Peepli live is my tribute to premchand: Anusha Rizvi. *Indian Express*. [online] Available at: http://archive.indianexpress.com/ news/peepli-live-is-my-tribute-to-premchand-anusha-rizvi/673746/ [Accessed 6 Apr. 2020].

Devasundaram, A. (2018). The subaltern screams: Migrant workers and the police station as spatio-carceral state of exception in the Tamil film *visaranai*. In: A. Devasundaram, ed., *Indian cinema beyond Bollywood: The new independent Indian cinema revolution*. New York: Routledge, pp. 257–280.

Devasundaram, A. (2021). Tracing Bergman in Contemporary Indian Cinema: Philosophical Cross-Connections in Through a Glass Darkly, Ship of Theseus and Dear Molly. In: H. Ford and D. Humphrey, eds., *Bergman World, Popular Communication, The International Journal of Media and Culture*, 19(2), 96–111. DOI: 10.1080/15405702.2020.1868046

Villarejo, A. (2018). Queer radiance: Margarita with a straw, disability and vision. In: A. Devasundaram, ed., *Indian cinema beyond Bollywood: The new independent cinema revolution*. New York: Routledge, pp. 66–77.

Conclusion

In a decade of evolution, the new wave of Indian Indies has transformed into a naturalised feature of contemporary Indian cinema, with increasingly prodigious output as reflected in the repositories of Netflix and Amazon Prime Video and the programmes of international film festivals. Significant impact of the digital and technological turn on Indie funding, exhibition and distribution will continue to influence filmmaking approaches, production culture and audience viewing practices in the foreseeable future.

The escalation of state regulation in the form of super censor laws and policing of film content on web streaming platforms foreshadows the spectre of filmmakers and digital service providers resorting to self-censorship to avoid exclusion. On the other hand, as envisioned by the Third Cinema manifesto, independent and dissenting counter-narratives conveyed through cinema become all the more indispensable in repressive authoritarian environments. The rising tide of majoritarian religious fundamentalism and amplifying state control of cinematic expression potentially could compel the Indian Indies to seek international pathways or devise new workarounds and innovative modes of production and representation. By that token, they would epitomise their classification as an 'independent' Indian new wave. There is abundant scope for expanded research on several specific facets of new Indian Indie cinema, from visual aesthetic strategies to digital production and distribution and audience reception. The intersectional ethos of the Indian Indies' thematic content paves a pathway to adventurous interdisciplinary analysis of these films, through the lens of politics, gender studies, queer theory, urban geography, Dalit perspectives and multifarious other disciplinary approaches.

DOI: 10.4324/9781003089001-8

Appendix
List of Indian Indie films

SERIAL NUMBER	FILM	YEAR
1	*Road, Movie*	2009
2	*The President Is Coming*	
3	*Sankat City*	
4	*Thanks Maa*	
5	*Madholal Keep Walking*	
6	*The Film Emotional Atyachar*	2010
7	*Bodhisatva*	
8	*Gandu*	
9	*I Am*	
10	*Udaan*	
11	*Road to Sangam*	
12	*That Girl in Yellow Boots*	
13	*LSD: Love Sex aur Dhokha*	
14	*Peepli Live*	
15	*Harud*	
16	*Dhobi Ghat*	
17	*Dekh Indian Circus*	2011
18	*Turning 30*	
19	*My Friend Pinto*	
20	*Satrangee Parachute*	
21	*Anhey Ghorey Da Daan/Alms for a Blind Horse*	
22	*B.A. Pass*	2012
23	*Peddlers*	
24	*Ship of Theseus*	
25	*Bumboo*	
26	*Jalpari*	
27	*Chittagong*	
28	*Filmistaan*	
29	*Shanghai*	
30	*Gangs of Wasseypur (1 and 2)*	
31	*Tasher Desh*	

(*Continued*)

(Continued)

SERIAL NUMBER	FILM	YEAR
32	*Miss Lovely*	
33	*Shahid*	
34	*Kahaani*	
35	*Paan Singh Tomar*	
36	*The Lunchbox*	2013
37	*Ankhon Dekhi*	
38	*Liar's Dice*	
39	*Listen . . . Amaya*	
40	*Monsoon Shootout*	
41	*Prague*	
42	*Rangrezz*	
43	*Anwar Ka Ajab Kissa (Sniffer)*	
44	*Local Kung Fu*	
45	*Lucia*	
46	*Fandry*	
47	*Papilio Buddha*	
48	*The Good Road*	
49	*Qissa: The Tale of a Lonely Ghost*	
50	*Margarita With a Straw*	2014
51	*Titli*	
52	*Court*	
53	*Keeda*	
54	*Lakshmi*	
55	*Asha Jaoar Majhe/Labour of Love*	
56	*Kaaka Muttai/The Crow's Egg*	
57	*Chauranga*	
58	*Teenkahon*	
59	*Killa/The Fort*	
60	*Unfreedom*	
61	*Haider*	
62	*Bangalore Days*	
63	*Masaan*	2015
64	*Gour Hari Dastaan: The Freedom File*	
65	*Parched*	
66	*Waiting*	
67	*Umrika*	
68	*Haraamkhor*	
69	*Island City*	
70	*Kaun Kitne Pani Mein*	
71	*Naanu Avanalla . . . Avalu/I Am Not He . . . I Am She*	
72	*Angry Indian Goddesses*	
73	*Loev*	
74	*Thithi*	
75	*Visaranai*	
76	*X: Past Is Present*	

SERIAL NUMBER	FILM	YEAR
77	*Tu Hai Mera Sunday*	2016
78	*Dhanak*	
79	*A Death in the Gunj*	
80	*Lipstick Under My Burkha*	
81	*Moh Maaya Money*	
82	*Dear Dad*	
83	*Budhia Singh: Born to Run*	
84	*Phobia*	
85	*Gurgaon*	
86	*Chidiya*	
87	*Sairat*	
88	*Trapped*	
89	*Lady of the Lake*	
90	*Aligarh*	
91	*Ka Bodyscapes*	
92	*Pink*	
93	*Raman Raghav 2.0*	
94	*Udta Punjab*	
95	*Anarkali of Aarah*	2017
96	*Poorna*	
97	*Beyond the Clouds*	
98	*In the Shadows*	
99	*Ribbon*	
100	*Mantra*	
101	*Jia aur Jia*	
102	*Sexy Durga*	
103	*Mukti Bhawan/Hotel Salvation*	
104	*Village Rockstars*	
105	*Kadvi Hawa*	
106	*Raag Desh*	
107	*Angamaly Diaries*	
108	*Tikli and Laxmi Bomb*	
109	*Newton*	
110	*Buddha.mov*	
111	*Rukh*	
112	*Ajji*	
113	*Angrezi mei kehte hain*	2018
114	*Manto*	
115	*Halka*	
116	*Mere Pyaare Prime Minister*	
117	*Kaalakaandi*	
118	*Bhavesh Joshi Superhero*	
119	*Mard ko dard nahin hota*	
120	*Soni*	
121	*Bulbul Can Sing*	
122	*Hamid*	
123	*Sir*	

(*Continued*)

(Continued)

SERIAL NUMBER	FILM	YEAR
124	Life of an Outcast	
125	Evening Shadows	
126	Sudani from Nigeria	
127	Dear Molly	
128	Ascharyachakit!	
129	Noblemen	
130	Manto	
131	Garbage	
132	Mehsampur	
133	Ek Aasha	
134	Bhonsle	
135	Side A & Side B	
136	#Gadhvi	2019
137	Posham Pa	
138	Bombairaiya	
139	Kamyaab	
140	Music Teacher	
141	Kattumaram/Catamaran	
142	Photograph	
143	Fireflies	
144	Dolly Kitty and Those Twinkling Stars	
145	Totta Pataaka Item Maal	
146	No Fathers in Kashmir	
147	Raahgir/The Wayfarers	
148	Moothon/The Elder One	
149	K.D.	
150	Kathaah@8	
151	Jallikattu	
152	Article 15	
153	Bulbbul	2020
154	Axone	
155	Ramprasad ki Tehrvi	
156	Chaman Bahar	
157	Serious Men	
158	The Disciple	
159	Sthalpuran/Chronicle of Space	
160	Chote Nawaab	
161	Manny	
162	Kalla Nottam/The False Eye	
163	Milestone	
164	Joji	2021
165	Toofan Mail	
166	Pebbles	
167	Seththumaan/Pig	
168	Ray	
169	The Great Indian Kitchen	
170	Sherni	
171	Pedro	
172	Dostojee/Two Friends	

Index

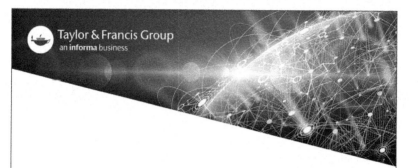